The Metan

a Heart

The Butterfly Effect
Greg Wilson

DEDICATION

Metamorphosis of a Heart is dedicated to the many Caterpillars that may think their lives are difficult, challenging or maybe even too much to bare, not realizing that they are destined to become butterflies. It's not about the things that happen to us in our lives, it's all about how we respond to those things. Hang in there, never give up, and know that soon enough you will be Free! Capable of Soaring and sharing a testimony about the very things you didn't think you could get past.

Contents

Greg Wilson

ACKNOWLEDGMENTS

God, Mom, and ALL of the people that has invested ANY time, thoughts, wisdom, advice, perspective, experiences, love, guidance and support that may have assisted me through the Metamorphosis of MY Heart. I am forever grateful, and humbled by your contribution. I hope you enjoy this expression.

I want to extend a Special Acknowledgement to Duane Taylor for assisting me with so many aspects of getting this book done. Thanks for introducing me to Colleen, who did a phenomenal job editing this project for me. Sean Milan, thanks for your support and for introducing Jasmine McCloud to me, who designed such an amazing book cover art.

My big brother Darrell Mitchell for your dedicated time, effort and expertise in making sure this project got published and completed.

The special few that took the time to read my book in advance to give me honest feedback to assure this book was good. Thank you so much, it means more than you know. Thanks for being apart of history!

PREFACE

My name is Harrison Gregory Heartland. Most people just call me Heart. When I was 13 years old someone told me I had an old soul and that I lived life as if I were twice my age. I don't know about that but I do know that I had to grow up quick. I had only myself to depend on. I'm not feeling sorry for myself, just reportin' the facts.

It also might simply be that I am a passionate person who has always felt in tune with his heart. One thing I've learned about being passionate is that passion brings both pleasure and pain. And pain comes at you in a lot of ways which can catch you off guard. With some people, it's the pain that comes after a loved one passes. For others pain comes when a close family member or friend disappoints, and for others pain comes from feeling passionate about living when all that surrounds you is despair. Some of my pain has come from the revelation that someone I loved and cherished was cheating on me and had decided that I just wasn't enough for him. That pain was especially unbearable. But like I say, pain can come at you hard when you least expect it.

Personal Facts: As I write this I am 33 years old. I was born in Panorama City, California. I am six feet two inches tall, weigh 225 pounds and have a medium-dark complexion. My eyes are brown, my hair is brown and I'm known for my intensity and for always smiling. My favorite food is EVERYTHING! I especially love spicy food like jambalaya. My hobbies are writing, music, photography, eating, traveling, meeting new people and helping people. The things about which I feel passionate are many. Love, making people happy, trying to heal other's hurts. I am often a bridge for people to get to where they need to go and I enjoy helping them.

As for my characteristics and personality traits, people often say that I'm sensitive, loyal, protective, a hopeless romantic, creative, a natural leader as well as submissive, trustworthy, honest, a great friend, kind-hearted, nice, considerate, hard-working, humorous and loving. That may all sound positive or normal or like I'm just a regular guy or maybe even bragging. That may be the case now but I haven't always been this guy. Life has fired some bullets at me like I was in the kill zone in Iraq or Anacostia in D.C.

What is that saying "no matter where you go, there you are?" Well here I am, I'm still standing and this is my story.

CHAPTER 1
First Thought - The Caterpillar

What do you remember most about your childhood? I recall a lot of moments quite vividly. I remember when I was a baby and felt as if this world hadn't a flaw. All I knew was this great expression of love, affection and attention I would get. It seemed like the only thing I was responsible for was crying at the proper times to indicate that I was hungry, needing my diaper changed, or when I was scared about something. At those times someone would come to my aid and tend to my needs. Wow, what if life was really like that? I swear with the innocence and lack of experience of a baby, the world was painted to be perfect, easy to navigate. It was gonna be alright, the world was a manageable place. I even think back to the feeling of everyone being excited to see me or wanting to hold me when I was a baby. Who knew with age, these things would change. Growing up meant that life was about to show me something completely different than that of being an innocent infant.

First, I learned that as life begins to evolve and develop the priorities and attention of things shift and change as well. Sometimes it can be drastic. I know for me, the shift and change of people's actions toward me and things that ceased to be priorities left me not understanding why, and it also led me to believe that people had stopped loving me or that I had done something wrong. I was not used to change. Early in my life I enjoyed consistency. Who knew that people wouldn't care the same or that

3

people's time and attention would be so much harder to come by as I became a young black man in America. The things that once were promises were now just my dreams, & stuff that I wished would happen. It's crazy how life goes, right?

Sometimes as I was growing up I felt like a little caterpillar. Caterpillars are like little mysteries, and much of the time you are not sure of how they will turn out. Like a baby, caterpillars start off small and maneuver their way through life by crawling. The beauty of it is that, no matter how small, how they are viewed or how often overlooked, they make it to their destination no matter how long it takes. Everything happens, as they say, "in God's time." You know the saying "you need to crawl before you walk?" Well the caterpillar's goal is to strive to fly and soar. In this case you have to crawl before you fly. It's the process of growing from caterpillar to butterfly that determines the fate and purpose of the caterpillar.

They call the process *metamorphosis* which means evolution. Before this takes place, caterpillars first must shed their old skin. As we are evolving and elevating to a new place in our lives, we must leave the person we were behind. Like the caterpillar, we are not meant to be the same human we were when we were little. The metamorphosis is so important and the change is so drastic for the caterpillar that the process usually causes them to lose their color and pattern. They usually appear shorter and different, and have no desire or interest in food during this time. Think about when you are going through a transition in your life. Many times, you may not even recognize yourself in the mirror. You may also find that the same things aren't fulfilling or pleasing to you. You go through a time of where you even lose the sense of what makes you happy, and what you desire. It's all a part of the process. We are the caterpillar going through the metamorphosis process.

What is the one thing each person in this world needs and longs for? Love! That's right, love. Some would argue that pain and/or loneliness are the opposite of love but my experience is that pain and loneliness and human cruelty lead you to love. Sounds like a movie made for the lifetime channel but I promise, that is how it happened to me.

If this were a Love Anonymous meeting I would admit the problem. That is the first step, right? I think it all started when I was just a little caterpillar and I grew up feeling loved without limits. Does that make sense? No limit to the amount of love I had access to. But I was limited by the number of people willing to share their love with me. I was even limited to the amount of love I felt I deserved because of the eventual lack of love that I received. I can't claim I understood the full essence of love as a kid, but I could surely tell the difference of having it and not having it. I learned that just because someone doesn't love me the way I wanted them to doesn't mean they weren't loving me with all they knew or had, I get it. I understand there's a level to love, and for each person it is defined differently and from each person it will look different or be expressed in different ways. This doesn't mean I should be sold short of it because for me love is like my lifeline, an essential element to my life. Without the love I needed I felt like I had no blood in my veins, no breath in my body, I felt like I was dying of deprivation.

I know what some people would do to feel loved. The things I would do to feel loved, wanted, appreciated, cherished, valued or simply seen were many. I spent most of my life feeling invisible, as if I was always a day late and a dollar short of the love I felt I deserved and wanted to attain. Love is not always something people experience or recognize, so once it is felt, it can become addicting or something truly longed for. A popular question is "is it better to have loved and lost, than to not have loved at all?" I say this speaks to how powerful it is. I also believe it is essential to everyone's life. Everyone needs love or to feel loved. Thankfully God is Love too 'because we humans kinda suck at it.

What if loneliness is the opposite of Love? There are so many people who have given up on life because of depression and/or loneliness. To me loneliness is like a disease, a disease that has emotional and mental symptoms that can cause uneasiness and sadness that may feel unbearable. It is like a disease that can have long term effects. It's also like one that some find the power and courage to beat and conquer. Why do so many people want to or long to be healed from it? Some would say love is the remedy. But what if that's not the case? Medicine is not always guaranteed to work and many don't speak about the side effects of Western drugs. Sometimes love could be the cause of this disease, so it's not wise to depend on love as the remedy or cure. At any rate that's just my theory.

Poetry

Love Ever Left You Feeling "Blue"
I feel like the clouds sittin' on sky blue
Sometimes cloud bright, sometimes grey
And no matter how long it takes
Eventually I'll find my way, so formless at times
So damn unclear
Yet whenever you look up I'm always here
I try to help redefine your definition of 'Blue'
And when you need I try to nourish you
When situations get too hot I try to protect you from
the rays
I'm like a cloud, these are my ways
The days I'm not present
You know I'm somewhere close
Most times overlooked, white like a ghost
Yet when I'm seen from the distances
People run for cover I'm just trying to get us to
reconnect with one another
But as I drift, I always end up single and expected
to feel free
I guess the sky I cover is an indication of me
"Blue," blue like the sky like the ocean
It's me without you like the berries like the bird…
you got me "Blue"
I've been sick for a long time and the loneliness
seems to have gotten worse over the years
I've been medicated with love by different doctors,
but for some reason the ache just never disappears
Maybe this disease is eternal, maybe without end

I think I may need a little more time for love
Give love a moment to see what it is truly capable
of
I know I wasn't created just to feel alone or
abandoned, misunderstood, unwanted, or worthless
I think it's time for me to embrace some change
Maybe it's the time and season for this little
caterpillar's metamorphosis
So here I am, shedding my skin, changing my form,
preparing for the changes
I am changing' and ready for the things that will
come.
Metamorphoses anyone?

CHAPTER 2
Changes...and a Love Flash-Back

Many caterpillars feed off of leaves, many times after they have fallen from the trees. Others only eat new leaves. To me this means some caterpillars are built to wait for the leaves to fall, meaning they're equipped with patience, but may not have the drive to do more than reach the things that are obvious. The sacrifice of freshness and better quality is okay, so as long as they get a chance to eat.

For others patience is shown through their ability to wait for the quality they are seeking. Putting in the time, energy and effort to climb to a level of a tree where they can eat and have access to fresh leaves that are still there green and hanging. To me this illustrates the fact that compromise is not always worth it. It also makes it much easier to settle oneself in a place where you will have endless access to fresh supply as opposed to gaining momentary pleasure by eating a leaf that has fallen, and then having to wait and hope for the next one to fall in order to have more nourishment. Insects are cold-blooded and their rate of development may be controlled by growing them at different temperatures. Darkness is necessary. As we humans strive for more knowledge and wisdom, we may also come to realize this world can be a cold dark place. If life experiences are the requirements for development, then we must embrace them differently if we want to survive and thrive.

I don't really know if I believe in mistakes. I do believe that situations and circumstances truly change us. Whether it redirects our paths, or gives us a new perspective we may not have known. We will find that it will determine some of the choices we will come to make as well. I believe that everything happens for a reason. Some things are lessons, some things are blessings, and some things make us stronger and better equipped for what's to come. God makes no mistakes - right? My Mother once told me the things we may not understand are all for reason and purpose. So when it comes to the point in my life where I feel my existence must've been a mistake, am I foolish to say such a thing?

I ask these questions often. It's hard to believe that people were created and meant to endure the kind of pain and hardship that I have experienced when other's lives are such that the only "struggle" in their vocabulary is when they're asking why their butler is dragging under the weight of their latest request. It's not that I question God, but I sometimes question the systems of human life in this world. Not a fair playing field where we're not all afforded the same opportunities and chances.

So I'm back to understanding mistakes vs. change. Is a mistake a mistake if we learn from it? Or are they enhancement tools that allow us the necessary push to activate changes in our lives? Why would God create me, and then leave or forsake me? All things have purpose and a place here on earth so I had to learn to grow from each experience. For instance, if I don't get something right the first time, instead of looking at it as a mistake, I look at it as an opportunity for a lesson to be learned. As I said I have always been told I'm an old soul in a young body. One lesson I've learned too many times in my short number of years on earth is that there are many forms of pain and learning that do not make pain good or right. It just means you have to endure to get to the other side.

It amazes me how someone can make you feel so alive, yet another time and another day can kill every bit of your being. It may be the worst feeling in the world to find you are with someone who makes you feel as if nothing or no one else matters and then in the next moment they destroy that feeling. Is this what love is supposed to be like? Is this what so many people fight so hard for? I guess I don't understand love, but I do understand pain.

FLASH-BACK, today is my eighth grade graduation, and all of the graduates are going to an after party tonight to celebrate the accomplishment of transitioning into high school. Everyone's excited, but I have something else I want to celebrate. Today was the first day that the girl I have been infatuated with for the past year and a half acknowledged my feelings, and agreed to be my girlfriend. I wrote her a letter and gave it to her before the graduation ceremony. I asked her to be my girlfriend, and for the first time, she actually wrote me back and agreed.

She handed me her letter after the ceremony with a beautiful smile on her face. I didn't know that letter and smile would change my life forever. It caught me by surprise because I was not what others considered attractive. I am tall and thin. I didn't have the best wardrobe, and I was always being made fun of in school for wearing the same clothes. I guess it's no surprise that though I knew everyone in the school, I wasn't all that popular. My popularity came from my association with my brother and cousin who went to the same school. Back to the letter: When she wrote "Yes, I'll be your girlfriend" I felt like my life had just begun.

I guess dreams do come true, because despite my shortcomings, I now had a girlfriend and she was simply beautiful. She was developed quite nicely for a 14 year-old. Her body was formed like an 18 year-old -- a perfect heart shaped ass, succulent breasts and hips. Even Beyoncé would be jealous. I swear she has a natural glow; smooth medium brown complexion that gave her the presence of an angel. She was 5'6" with long curly dark-brown hair. She had the most beautiful eyes ever created, and a personality that would make flowers bloom in the winter, a beauty that would make rain fall in summer, and a smile that made sunshine look dull. She was the most beautiful girl I'd ever seen and I couldn't believe she agreed to be with me. I had never been more excited in my life and I couldn't wait to go to the party that night, especially because her best friend was hosting it and I knew that my new girlfriend would be the light of the party. How had I gotten so lucky in love?

I was at home ironing and laying my clothes out. I had found a new way to recycle the clothes I had so they wouldn't look like the same exact outfit everyone saw me wear the week before. I cleaned my only pair of shoes and I even went to the 99 cents store to get new cologne to wear that night, so I could smell good when I got close to my baby. If everything were to go as planned, I might get a kiss, which reminded me that I forgot to buy gum at the 99 cents store, so I carried a travel-sized tube of toothpaste in my pocket so I could be fresh when I went in for my kiss.

I was so ready, so excited to see my angel. I couldn't help but to wonder what she would be wearing, if she would be happy to see me, if she would dance with me (I should've practiced my moves in the mirror a little more!), and I hoped she'd give me a kiss. Tonight was the night, it had to be. Everything was working out in my favor-- finally. Even my mom was willing to drop my brother, cousin and me off at the party. Her only rule was that we would have to stay and come home together.

So here we were walking into the party, and my heart was racing like I was in a track meet and this was the last leg of the 400 meter relay. I walked around and said hello to everyone. I was so excited to see my girlfriend, it didn't even bother me that everyone ignored me and acted as if I didn't exist. After walking around for about 20 minutes, I realized that she wasn't there. I located her best friend and asked her if she knew where the love of my life was, and she didn't seem too excited about my inquiry, because her response was simply "I don't know." I thought she was kind of rude, but nobody was going to mess up my night.

Two hours later, I was sitting in the same spot, guarding the door waiting for her to walk into the party, but I started to wonder if she was even going to come. I stopped fighting my body's request and went to use the bathroom. This was a task in itself because every bathroom was occupied with people making out and getting their kissing in for the night. The kiss I had been fantasizing about for a year and a half. After returning from the bathroom, I noticed the most beautiful girl in the world was on the dance floor, and I couldn't contain my excitement. I began taking steps towards her so I could greet my girlfriend with a hug, but what followed my first three steps in pursuit of that hug was a glimpse of reality.

Reality was that she was dancing with and hugging up on a high school boy who was rumored to be her ex- boyfriend. They were laughing, and dancing, and kissing. I was confused. Why would she tell me she would be my girlfriend, and then have this guy interfere? I wanted some answers and I wanted them now. So I approached her, and I tapped her on her shoulder and said
"Hey, can I talk to you?" She responded, "Ok, give me a few minutes."

A few minutes became half 'n hour, and then her best friend approached me and said,
"Look, I don't know why you would think she would want to be with someone like you. I am the one that wrote you back. I thought it was a joke. She has a man, so get it out of your mind. You will never be her man. Look at you." Then this girl started laughing.

After her best friend said that to me, she whispered to the one I thought was my girl, and both of them started to look at me and laugh so hard, it looked like they were about to pee on themselves. I felt my eyes begin to water and then as I tried to head outside to get some fresh air, my brother came up to me and started laughing at me. It seems everyone in the party and at the school were amused by my attempt and found it to be the joke of the night. I became the laughing stock of the graduation party.

I had to get out of there. I could not stay. I needed to go for a walk to get my emotions under control. Once I got outside, I just burst into tears. I felt so stupid for believing anyone would want to be with me. I felt so alone, so depressed, so small. I decided it would be best for me to go on a long walk. It's not that anyone would even notice that I was gone. I needed to cool off. I needed time to think, a few moments to be alone.

I went for that walk and from that point on my whole life changed. I knew I was supposed to wait for my cousin and brother before leaving the party and that my mom said she would come pick us up at 1:00 AM. I was too embarrassed to return to the party, so I left. I didn't know where I was going but I was deeply hurt and needed to get far away from the cruelty of my sad reality.

I began walking. I was in my own world, a world where I was important as I was trying to work through what had happened that day and evening. After a while I kind of noticed this one car kept passing me. Back and forth. Back and forth. This made me more than a little nervous, so I decided to just head home. Palmdale California is a pretty wide-spread city, so I knew this walk was a mission in itself, but I was determined to take it on and get away from the pain I had just endured. But I noticed the white car kept passing by. I ignored it and kept on walking. I was so hurt. I couldn't believe my girl's best friend would do such a thing to me. Nor that my angel was no longer so angelic. She seemed so nice. I would've never imagined her being a part of such a terrible prank. How could she do such a thing? In my mind I just kept seeing her laugh at me. It shattered every piece of my heart and gravely wounded my self-esteem. I was so broken, not even super glue could put me back together.

Twenty minutes into my walk, I began thinking of a plan just in case the people in the car tried something because though I was deep in thought, I couldn't help but notice that every five minutes they would find a way to pass by me again. They just didn't know they would be messing with the wrong person. They caught me on a bad night and there was no telling what I would do. I figured I wanted to be smart because you have to be prepared in a situation like this. Of course when a "situation" takes place nothing ever goes as planned.

The car pulled up beside me as I was about to cut through the desert and two dark-skinned black men— one short and one taller, both older scruffy and unattractive — stopped the car and asked me," Excuse us, do you know how to get to Palmdale Boulevard?"

I sighed instantly with relief thinking "Okay these people were just lost so I turned around to point in the correct direction to Palmdale Boulevard. As I turned back around, the short one was out of the car and right in front of me with a little shiny silver gun to my ribs! Tears started forming in my eyes immediately. I was in shock. I had never seen a real gun before and someone was going to use it on me. In my mind all I could think was, "really, after the night I've had? Why me? I thought my life couldn't get any worse than the humiliation I had suffered at the party."

The short one yelled, "Get in the car!" and he pushed me towards the open back door. At first I just stood there crying he repeated his demand shoving the gun into my ribs again. I got in the car. The short one got in the back seat with me. I was crying hysterically. He said,
"If you just shut up I might change my mind about killing you." The taller one was driving. He cut off the short one saying,
"Make him shut up!"

The short one said,
"Oh yeah, I know how to make him shut up," and began to pull his pants down with his right hand while holding the gun with his left. When he got his pants down near his knees, he told me to suck on his dick. He said
"This will shut your ass up." He began shoving my head down into his lap and forcing me to choke on his dick as my tears rolled uncontrollably down my cheeks. I had every intention of just biting the shit out of it but soon as the thought rushed into my mind, he put the gun to my head and said "don't try anything stupid, I will shoot your ass! Believe me." The next thing I felt was the car stopping. I tried lifting my head to see where we were but he pushed my head down hard jamming his dick half down my throat and said, "You better put your head down and keep sucking!

Furiously, the driver got out of the driver's seat and jerked opened the back door. With the door open he forced my pants off and tried jamming himself inside me. I turned around and tried to fight him off but he punched me in the mouth and continued to hit me in the ribs and the back of my head until the guy with the gun used brute force to turn my head to make me keep sucking his dick. The driver then jammed his erect penis inside of me. Rough, dry and unprotected. My continuous bleeding didn't make him stop at all. It actually made him push in and out even more.

As I cried and screamed, the guy with the gun jammed his penis down my throat while the other guy continued to shove his dick in my ass. I cried. I screamed. When the short one ejaculated, he made sure to cum all over my face. They both laughed. I was dazed. I didn't know what to do. I was scared, hurt, in pain, screaming, crying. I was in the middle of who knows where. It all happened so fast. No way I would make it out of this alive. Even though I was screaming as loud as I could, I knew nobody would hear me. Deep inside I knew my screaming was pointless.

They drove me to a desert not far from where they picked me up. It is a place I'll never forget. There was nothing and no one around. The pain and shame of being raped by two men was nearly unbearable. I was bleeding like a wounded animal. I cried so much, tears wouldn't even come out anymore. Only sound. I felt as if all my pride and what was left of my self-esteem were ripped away. No one could ever know what had just happened to me. What would people say? Would anyone even believe me? I wasn't supposed to have left the party alone. My mother would be so mad.

After the two men relieved themselves, they pushed me out of the car bare and exposed. They left me sitting helplessly in the desert. I cried so much that I must've laid there crying for an hour. I was surprised to be alive, but the way I felt I may as well have been dead. As I gathered the strength to get up and walk out of the desert, I regained my focus about what just happened. I was there with nothing on bleeding, dirty, in pain, semen all over my face and inside of me. I began putting my clothes on. I knew I had to get away from that spot before these guys returned to kill me.

As I got back to the main street, I realized I was much closer to the party than I was home, so I limped my way to a gas station. In the filthy station restroom I cleaned myself up a bit and headed back to the party. I knew I couldn't go back inside, especially now that my underwear was soaked with blood. My clothes were so dirty. I couldn't bear any more embarrassment. I made my way back to the house where the party was being held before my mom came to pick us up. I just sat outside and tried to hold in my tears. Even worse, no one had even noticed I'd been gone.

As people walked out of the party, they would throw a smile my way, not to be cordial, but to get one last laugh at me as they left. I cried silently all the way home. I couldn't even sit down all the way. I don't know if the situation itself hurt the most or the fact that my mother didn't even realize or care to acknowledge that something was clearly wrong with me. She asked how the party had been and I couldn't even mumble a reply, but she didn't seem to care and proceeded to drive my brother cousin and me home.

There are many forms of pain and ways that a body can ache. As I looked through blurred eyes I couldn't stop crying. When I got home I went straight to the shower and couldn't help but notice the stream of blood flowing down the bathtub drain. I was attempting to wash off the pain and hurt. I scrubbed harder and harder in attempt to wash off the feeling of violation that enveloped me and the shame I felt for having let those men do such a thing to me. The flashes of thought made me cringe. I could hear the sickening sound of my own screams and I could see, as though I were hovering above the scene of the crime, my own rape and my attempts to fight back. I couldn't help but to feel shame, guilt and disappointment. I wasn't a real man because I didn't fight hard enough. I must not be a man because I couldn't stop two men forcing themselves into me. As I took a long shower, the nightmare of what had happened became more and more painful. My body burned like someone was pouring hot water all over me. I suffered from this pain long after this night, not only mentally and emotionally, but physically too. It hurt me when I walked for almost a month. Every time I used the bathroom, blood found its way in the toilet too. I feel like I was never the same from that night on. I was changed. I was scared, ashamed, and embarrassed. And I couldn't even clearly remember what the assholes looked like.

Ever since that night it's been hard for me to allow anyone to get close with me. For a while I'd flinch if someone tapped me on the shoulder. It's like living in a nightmare while you are awake. Over and over I would remember that gun, the pain of their penetration and the sounds of them yelling at me. I could not shake an eerie, queasy feeling I had about Palmdale. I didn't like to go anywhere from my house alone. I didn't know if the two men had seen me and followed me because they knew where I lived. It was all so scary to me. I mean if their paths crossed mine again how would I know who they are? But they might know me. That scared me so much. I felt so worthless. It made me think that nobody would ever respect me after that. I felt like I should just die. My life wasn't any good anyway. I wished I could start my young life over. Maybe I'd be loved if I did something different.

I felt as if nobody cared about me. I officially began an "I don't care what happens to me" stage of my life. It was an internal battle. I tried to overpower the pain I felt by inflicting different types of pain on myself. I didn't know what else to do. I didn't want to live like this. I didn't want to feel like this every day of my life. I simply thought ending my life was the solution so I began elaborately contemplating suicide.

Sometimes it's the unspoken words and unanswered questions that hold the most wisdom within them. After going through such an unbearable level of heartache and disappointment, and feeling as if no one in the world cared about me or even paid enough attention to me to acknowledge my existence, I really thought things would be much easier if I wasn't here. I became fixated with the idea of dying, and I would imagine what it would be like. I found myself planning my entire funeral from beginning to end and the only curiosity I had was who would even show up. I felt invisible. I felt like I didn't belong or as if I wasn't wanted. I felt like a joke or a big mistake. I couldn't do anything right, no matter how much I tried to over compensate and make it right.

Poetry

What Should I Do?
Today is the day in which I won't see another
The sun will stop shining and birds won't fly any further
I will never see another face
Won't feel the need to go any place
I can't live any more for there is no reason
I tried to like myself, every day- every season
But there just seems to be the least bit of hope
When I look for love- do I see any? Nope.
They say they love me but why doesn't it show?
Would they love me any more if I decided to go?
I guess I don't care when it's my time to die
And again they may accuse me of telling a lie
I wanted to live to see where life would lead me to
Would it lead me to love? Well maybe, but not from you.
I go to school every-day to get my education.
For some reason it doesn't fulfill my mom's expectations.
I try and I cry hoping things will get better, but "no," instead I end up causing myself to upset her
I don't know, God, tell me what should I do?

Should I die today and not finish up school?
Or should I keep feeling depressed and cause myself
to be stressed?
Or is it another choice that you feel would be the
best?
Until you give me an answer my feelings will stay on
my chest if no answer is given soon "in peace I will
rest."
There's just so many questions...

CHAPTER 3
Questions

Sometimes when the temperature rises or falls we have to adjust. The adjustments allow us to cope, deal or function despite discomfort. If the temperature isn't right, it doesn't mean we will not grow; it just may stump or delay our development. When in darkness, any bit of light becomes our focus. When we feel we are in a dark place, it is much easier for God to reveal himself to us and also for us to be clear about what it is we are supposed to be aware of when it comes. What's interesting about darkness is that it is necessary for development, and for us, darkness is instrumental in our ability to reflect and see where changes need to be made. Darkness allows focus as well. And most times when in darkness we find there will not be many others around us to give support. It has been my unfortunate experience that not many people will associate with you through your development process, so it weeds out who is meant to transition along with you in your life.

Like most typical teenagers, I made mistakes. I found that at home I was always getting yelled at or getting in trouble, and many times I would feel as if I was in the way, like I was just a waste of space. I felt my brother was being treated better than I was, and my cousin was being favored over me. They must've known it too, because they would tease me about it. After a few months of feeling invisible, I wanted to make that a reality. I wanted to disappear. I felt it would be convenient for everyone and it would make everyone happier.

I dwelled obsessively on my contemplation of suicide. This seemed to be an option that would eliminate pain, hurt, disappointment, and it would mean that I wouldn't have to live any longer feeling so miserable. I needed a getaway, a retreat. By the way it seemed no one gave a damn anyways, so why not disappear. I thought about this for some time and I even had to configure how I thought my death would go or play out.

Poetry

My Time to Go!
Is it really the end? Is it really all over today?
How come the people that would talk shit
Don't have anything more to say?
Don't cry please don't shed any tears
You wonder why 'cause it's the beginning of my golden years
Life was okay but now it's no longer here
All this sadness in my heart
Death was something not feared, I was ready to go
I couldn't deal with much more pain
Why go on with this life when I have nothing to gain
As I lay here in a coffin I begin to wonder why
So many people look over me with crystal tears in their eye
it's not a bad thing
Why can't they just laugh and smile
I've been looking forward to this day
For quite a while
I know you'll miss me
But don't you say goodbye

I'll see you when you get there
To the heavens in the sky
I lived a difficult life believe me it was bad
Pain and heartaches became the only feelings I had
Now I have no troubles to look forward to
I don't have to tolerate people that aren't even true
I'm still with you so don't you ever forget about me
Now when I close my eyes
Never again will I see
So long sorrows
And good-bye heartaches
I don't have to worry
About making any more mistakes
My life was fucked up
About that there's no doubt
Now I have nothing else to worry about
Damn I look good in this suit and tie
Why is it so hard for you to say good-bye?
Don't cry too much
You'll see me again one day
Remember my smile
And the words I would say
Don't be frightened
By me laying here stiff
What if I were happy with my life?
Would I still be here?
What if? I can't have you all feeling sympathetic for
me
Close my coffin- put me 6 feet under and let me be
I can't bear to hear
Another one of your sad good-bye songs
You're making my soul sad
Because I feel I've done you all wrong
Leave me alone!
Why can't you hear my damn plea?

You're making me sad by all the memories
You're instilling inside of me
Okay I'm beginning to regret it
I'm not going to lie
I shouldn't have left the ones who loved me
Why did I have to die?
My life may have seemed bad
But maybe it was better than I thought
Many have done me wrong
But the ones that loved me I had forgot
I'm sorry
Please forgive me for taking my own life
If you were in my shoes
You'd probably make the same sacrifice
It's hard to live as a troubled young teen
All these people don't understand me
Is that a reason for them to be so mean?
All their comments and opinions
Brought my pride low
Sorry everybody
It really felt like my time to go.
Good-bye.

Well, let me say this: suicide wasn't for me. I
tried and I just think it wasn't meant for me. I know
that I overthink everything, and by the time my
thoughts get going, thankfully logic starts to come in
there somewhere too. I'm not going to cut myself,
'cause I freak out when I see blood so I wouldn't even
allow a knife that type of access. Suicide by knife -
that was out. I thought about running into the middle
of the street, but I watched too many movies of
someone living through a collision with a car and
having to live life as a vegetable. I knew I would be
more miserable if I ran in front of a car and didn't die. I
was terrified of guns after what happened to me, so I

wasn't going to shoot myself. But I did have two ideas.

One idea was that I was determined to drink a cup of bleach. I knew this surely had to work, so I began by taking a little sip and I swear that's all it took for me to be extremely sick for like four days throwing up over and over. Bleach was now out I had to think of another option.

A month or so later I remember feeling horribly depressed. The trigger was that I got into trouble for something that I didn't do. My frustration and sadness grew. I remember trying to talk to my mom about the situation and how I felt, but it seemed she didn't hear me and wouldn't try to understand my perspective so I stopped caring. I stopped caring about that incident, myself, and everything around me. I remember rushing into my mom's cabinet to grab the bottle of aspirin that was there, and I attempted to make my next suicide attempt.

Overdosing with aspirin also didn't go well. I ended up getting sick, and throwing up for almost 30 minutes straight after ingesting the tablets. I hadn't thought this all the way through. Honestly, I think subconsciously, I just wanted my mom or someone to see me trying to kill myself and hug me and tell me they loved me. Though that didn't happen, I knew in the back of my mind that it wasn't meant for me to take my life after all. I didn't have enough balls to kill myself. I cared too much to not care (if that makes any sense).

Then one day I remember I was laying on the

living room floor after school. I felt alone, invisible, misunderstood, unloved, unwanted, and I didn't know why I just couldn't stop crying. I felt an undefined pain. I felt so much sadness and emptiness inside. I had nothing but questions for God. I couldn't stop asking, "Why did you want me here? What am I supposed to do with this life? Does anyone love me? Would anyone miss me if I died? Why do I feel so sad? Does anyone care? Does anyone even know I am here? Why do I feel so invisible? Does anyone get me?"

I continued with my questioning, "God....please send me a sign to let me know you hear me." I questioned my self-worth my purpose, my relevance, everything. I didn't have the motivation to even get up and get on with my life from day to day. Life became a gigantic obligation, not something I enjoyed living. I lost all sense of happiness and fulfillment. I felt as if I lost all my strength and power and my will to go on.

Certain situations can destroy us if we give them that power. For me, at this particular time in my life, I didn't feel valued, I didn't have much and I felt the little dignity I had left had been stolen from me. To be at the point where you believe you cannot ever feel any worse or be any lower is a devastating feeling of hopelessness especially for a young black teen with limited resources. It's not a feeling I would wish upon anyone. As I look back at that time now I realize that it took all that for me to appreciate what was eventually to come in my life. At that point in my life I had to start again, I had to crawl out of that deep dark hole to regain my sense of self and to reclaim my internal power -- my life's engine so to speak.

Sometimes I have felt limited due to circumstances or experiences, but what I have had to realize is that sometimes all of the answers lie within the question. Many times I have found that if I ask the right questions, the right things will be revealed. Life can be like a riddle or a puzzle. It takes time, but once you get the hang of it, the bigger picture may be revealed and the connections of one thing to another are made much clearer.

I found that we all have the tools and power to get through any situation. It is how we use the tools and resources we are given that determines the how complicated or easy our journey is. So when I ask questions I know I must configure what it is that I need in order to discover the answer. Sometimes I find wisdom in the process, but not always in the answer. Sometimes I don't necessarily get the answers to the questions I ask, but it's important that I realize that it's not because an answer isn't coming. It's because there's something that I am meant to learn from the situation.

When I've gone through challenging times, I naturally have looked for or sought support or comfort from another person. Through many difficult times in my life, I had to actively seek out support systems or guidance because they were readily available to me or easy for me to identify. I realized that I had lived so much of my life to meet the standards or needs of what other people wanted me to be. But once I understood and started living my own truth, I found that there was no one around to embrace, accept or affirm me. I know I have friends, and I know I have family who care about me, but truthfully everyone has their own baggage and their own issues, so for me to expect them to willingly grab hold of my problems and help me out was unrealistic.

I also can't pretend that everyone knew what I was going through, so I can't even be mad of the lack of response to my request for help. I didn't feel deserving of love because I didn't even love myself. Why should I? People would look at me and just think I was weird or trying to find myself. Though these things may have been true, I was also battling with whether I wanted to live or die.

I learned that I didn't understand my own true capabilities or strength until I was put in a position where I was required to understand my inner strength. I didn't know what the next day would bring. I felt no one would understand me, because even I didn't understand me. The few times I tried to open up and ask for help, I felt rejected. I felt like support was not provided and no one really wanted to look deeper into my pain to understand.

Family= Blood, Friends=Water
They say blood is thicker than water
I believe this statement is true because blood can stain
It's not something that people can survive without
But it usually means wounds and pain has been inflicted when it's around
On the flip-side, it's always with/within you
Water is something that brings momentary refreshment but it can eventually leave you to thirst once again
Water is used at times to assist, refresh, nourish and

help things grow
It's essential to life, but in a different way
There's been many times in my life I depended on my
water and treated it as blood
And there were times I had to dilute my blood with
water
Why is that?

I grew up feeling uncomfortable, odd and different, and as if I didn't fit in or was misunderstood. I felt like I could do no right and that I was always being judged by my family. When I was little I would always put in extra effort to be the most helpful and gracious kid, kinda like I was trying to earn my place. But I could never make everyone happy. Of course.

The process of evolution, change and metamorphosis can be quite emotional. But what is life without it? It helps us build and gain strength. It helps us grow. I used to think change was something that worked against me, but I began to embrace it because I began to appreciate the things it would finally reveal. I learned a lot of life lessons through the changes I encountered when it came to family, friendships, and even how I am expected to conduct my life.

I remember times I would cry to my mom and she would teach me the wonderful life lessons that aren't easy to come by that would help me develop tough skin. As I've come of age I realized that it wasn't until I loved myself that I started being myself without apologizing. I also started building stronger relationships with my family and started experiencing real happiness within me. Momma never told me life would be like this, but I know she would have if she could have.

CHAPTER 4
If I Could

If I knew then what I know now, there's a lot of my life for which I would've been better prepared. It's crazy, I'm saying that, but then I also wonder where I would be or who I would be if I hadn't been through some of the things that I have gone through.

I learned early on not to live with regret, so I became pretty good at rolling with the punches, and dealing with the cards that were dealt. I don't know if I had encountered so much pain that I became numb to a lot of it, or if I had just become more resigned in my responses to the things that I could not change.

I learned so much from watching my mother while I was growing up. She is one person I saw make something out of very little, and I swear you would never see her sweat. Her resilience is where I believe my pattern came from. She taught me so much and made sure I needed for nothing. My mother taught me about appreciation, that it's the little things that matter the most. She was my prime example of graciousness. Throughout her life she remained humble, caring for others and treating people good all the time. My mother was not materialistic — a wonderful trait that allowed her to make sure I was always provided for.

My mother has made me come to appreciate the true essence of sacrifice. Now here I am truly experiencing the hardships that life keeps bringing my way, and I feel as if I had been abandoned having to deal and fend for myself. Maybe it's just apart of growing up or instrumental in learning and growing to become who I am expected to become. But how do you grow into the person your destined to be if the experiences kill you along the way?

I now realize that it was childlike to assume that my mom was some type of superhero who could shield me from all heartache and pain. I viewed her as if she were created to help me through my life's journey, while forgetting at times that she was a person living her own life as well. I grew up feeling at times that I was invisible, over-looked or unloved, but as time went on I've come to realize just how much love, support and sacrifice I was provided. Just because someone doesn't love you the way you expect or want them to love you doesn't mean they aren't loving you with all they've got, the best they know how.

I honestly can say the happiest times of my life was when I was very young and it was just me and her. Growing up I felt like life was an adventure. From an adult perspective I would call it survival in the wild. I don't know how my mom did it, but she surely did, and I truly love and appreciate her for showing me what everlasting love is.

For the first five years of my life, it was just me and my mom. During those formative years I learned how to access my own vivid imagination and find my own inner peace and solitude. I still use these "life tools" today. Even at a young age, I remember being a kid that many kids wanted to play with, but I choose not to be bothered because I would much rather be alone, another thing I brought into my adulthood. I never really had a lot of friends, but the very few I made were important to me. I have always been ultra-sensitive and always in tune with my emotions. My cousins used to make fun of me because I would cry a lot. My feelings would get hurt so easily. These things have also toughened my skin for adulthood.

When I was little my mom heard a song sung by Regina Belle called *If I Could*[1] and she dedicated it to me. As I have come of age, every time I listen to this song, it brings me to tears. I remember on my last birthday, after spending the day with my mom, the song happened to come on the radio, which was only a sign that God was with us, and that He was co-signing the moment of love and connection with his own love and connection to us. The timing couldn't have been more perfect. I wouldn't trade that day or that moment, as my mother and I both made our very best effort at singing along with the song. Despite the nontraditional formations of our voices, it still sounded like it was in the perfect key and to my ears our pitch was perfect. Perfect day, perfect weather, perfect company, perfect song, — perfect moment.

I remember my mom was always protective over me and also everyone in our family. Though we have truly had our challenges and ups and downs she would never let anything happen to me. I truly am blessed to have the mother I have, and to think of how selfless she is, it makes me emotional. Let me share with you the lyrics to the Regina Belle song my mom dedicated to me.

If I Could

---

[1] *If I Could,* words and music by Ron Miller, Ken Hirsch, and Sharron Marti. Published by Sony/ATV Music Publishing LLC, Warner/Chappell Music, Inc., Universal Music Publishing Group. Recorded by Regina Belle. Released 1993.

If I could I'd protect you from the sadness in your eyes
Give you courage in a world of compromise
Yes I would if I could
I would teach you all the things I've never learned and
I'd help you cross the bridges that I've burned
Yes I would if I could
I would shield you from your innocence from time
But the part of life I gave you isn't mines
I'll watch you grow so I can let you go if I could
I would help you make it through the hungry years
But I know I could never cry your tears,
Babe but I would If I could
If I could in a time or place where you don't wanna be
You don't have to walk along this road with me
My yesterday won't have to be your way
If I Knew I'd try to change the world I brought you to
Now there isn't much more that I can do but I would If
I could
If I could I would try to shield your innocence from
time
But the part of life I gave you isn't mine
I'll watch you grow so I can let you go
If I could I'd help you make it through the hungry
years
But I know that I can never cry your tears
But I would if I could.

I am sure that most mothers would want to
shield and protect their children from the cruelty of
this world. I know my mom had no idea about the
things I would go through or the challenges I would
face during my lifetime. It still shocks me when I think
about the things I had to fight and how God
strengthened me enough to make it through. Rapists,
abusers, racial walls and homophobic barriers all

attempted to block my path. But I truly am blessed and grateful because I have made it.

I thank my mom for trying to protect me. She tried to save me, guard me and keep me from the hardships and the harshness of this world but she had a life and her own things to deal with. She couldn't watch me 24/7, and in order to truly understand the essence of life I had to experience and learn from everything every day.

I love, love. Love is something I have always longed, yes ached for. I know my mom loves me. I grew up questioning the love shown by others because even as a kid for some reason, I felt like the ugly duckling of my family. I felt I was the one that was last thought of or looked at, the one that didn't really belong. Maybe it was all in my mind, but that feeling was carried with me for years, all the way through to adulthood. In time I came to realize that people don't love the same, and each person's expression is unique.

Just because a person doesn't love you the way you want them to doesn't mean that person isn't loving you with everything he or she has got or in the best way they know how. I found this to be true though it doesn't mean that I should accept a minimalist version of someone's attempt to love me. I deserve to be loved in a way that is best for me. So what is Love? As I said, each person defines it differently. But I do know that it is something so powerful that everyone longs to have it, to feel it and attain it. It's like a drug. And if love is a drug then I think I am addicted.

Poetry

Hello My Name Is...
And I'm addicted to
Well, how am I to explain it?
All I can say is you
'Cause out the blue
Like a joint
You were passing through my finger-tips
Only to stimulate me
As you ran across my lips
I had to inhale you because I wanted to
Become one with your nature
Something I have come to love so quickly
Now I can't help but hate ya
Nobody ever told me
You'd have my head up in the clouds
So high in the sky
I don't know if I could ever come down
This feeling so serene
I must come clean
I never felt this way before
I'm conflicted
I feel like a fiend looking for my next thing
But you've got me restricted.
I'm an addict, I need a doctor
Or someone to intervene
You're a drug
I need a "hit" of love
And it's a helluva thing
Going through withdrawal
You are the cause
Of this struggle I now face
You are my drug

Now depriving me of this substance I must taste
You can't get me drunk or tipsy
Then take away my cup
You get me addicted
Then deprive me
Now I can't get enough
Can I get a refill?
Better yet I'll pop some pills trying to numb this pain
It's like I hit rock bottom or need some type of asylum
'Cause it's driving me insane
I'd rather be sober than allow myself to be under the
influence again
Because love can have you stuck
Down on your luck
And you'll be in denial that it came to an end
Love, why am I still addicted to you?

What happens when you have no access to the
very thing you're addicted to? Some go through
withdrawals and can even die because of their body's
dependency on it. My heart depends on this addiction.
As you may know, when you're addicted to
something, you would do many things for it. Let's say
love for example. I have found myself doing things I
never thought I would do. Dating people I knew
weren't good for me, allowing myself to be accessible
to people who weren't even deserving to be within my
arms reach, and most of all letting down my guard to
the wrong individuals for the wrong reasons.
Sometimes I feel like I need Rehab.

All in the pursuit of love. When I couldn't find it, it
left me feeling even emptier. Have you ever felt that
way? Or on the flip side, I experienced finding that
person who took my breath away and showed me

new ways of love that I never even realized were possible. The feeling that left me speechless yet feeling as if I had so much I wanted to say. It made my body tingle to be given even a mere touch. Have you ever met the kind of person who comes along and sweeps you off your feet to a point that you cannot even concentrate because every thought you have is dedicated to that person?

I've had this feeling it left me waiting for my next 'high', my next 'hit' of love. Have you ever fallen this hard in love? I felt like I couldn't be caught when I was starting to fall in love. At times I fell with an awful thud and couldn't get up. Other times it was not too hard to get up and recuperate, but the point of the matter is that I fell. Sometimes it left me wounded and bruised, but I healed.

What I would do after the fall is what matters. Do I stay down, or do I get up? If someone truly cares about you, should they fall with you? Or should they leave you alone on the ground to figure it out for yourself? What if they are not ready to fall? Or what if they can maintain their stance and balance much better than you and they never fall, what does that mean? Does that mean they don't love you? Does it mean they are strong, capable of catching you as you fall so that they can assure you are protected so you don't get hurt?

Well I have tough skin. I love hard and I am not afraid to fall. I have learned from my previous mistakes and I know that tomorrow is not promised to any of us, so why live based on what ifs or false hopes or unclear dreams that may never come true. I learned to live, love and trust myself to do it. I can't be mad at anyone if they can't love me. I'm a lot to Love.

I love me, and I have fallen deeper and deeper in love with myself, and I am infatuated with me, to the point where I cannot get enough. I no longer feel incomplete, as long as I always have me. God has blessed me so much. So I praise him in everything I do. If he has me fall it's for me to pray up to him for blessing me the ways that He has. I cry, but I allow those tears to be of joy because the Lord has protected me through all my hard times and new situations. I admit, I can't say I feel this confident every single day, but the days I don't I access the reasons I have found to love myself and to recognize how blessed I am. I am a work in progress, but willing to do as much over time that's necessary. Before I found this inner strength I would've been broken and torn, but have I learned how to keep it moving. One of my last attempts at love and relationship was truly a learning experience. It taught me a lot about boundaries, tolerance, trusting myself and following my instincts.

You know what's interesting? Honestly, most parents don't hope or wish their child will end up being gay. This is actually something I find that most parents pray about or if they're small minded, may think is a curse or karma for something they did to someone in the past. So of course most parents raise their children based upon societal thinking or concepts.

Growing up, I don't recall having many conversations about sex. Now my mom is the type who if she believed something was going on, she was gonna come up in the room and give you some condoms and ask you if you're having sex, and if so, to make sure you don't bring no nappy headed kids up in the house with snotty noses and tears in their eyes. I love that my mom always made sure lines of communications were there, but what do you do with a kid like me? I seemed like a kid who would end up being a 40 year old virgin because I was so socially awkward. I was the quiet kid that was always locked up in his room writing or listening to Monica's music.

My mom never had to pop up in my room with condoms talking 'bout don't get no girl pregnant, 'cause she knew that wasn't an issue I was having. Mind you I had that big crush on that beautiful girl in eighth grade and I had other female crushes. I even had my share of girlfriends but I was the type that would break up with her once she started expecting me to have sex with her or do more than kissing and touching. I like guys. This was something I think I realized at an early age, but didn't explore until I was around 15 or 16. I believe I liked girls also, but guys seemed to capture my attention much more.

I remember my first time I acknowledged my attraction to another boy, I was actually around seven or eight years old. I remember it was me, my dad and brother inside of Mervyns' Department Store and I saw this little boy who had to be like 11 years old, and I remember saying after he walked by "he is cute!" Before I could turn all the way around, I remember getting slapped in my mouth and being told "boys don't call boys cute!" One thing is for certain, I didn't say that again. I kept opinions to myself. It didn't stop me from thinking it though. Clearly there are always expectations about what it means to be a man and being gay was definitely viewed as a weakness that made you less of a man. I knew at that point it wasn't something everyone would be okay with, so I just kept it deep inside.

I think I really began exploring my emotions much more in the sixth grade. I recall having my first major crush on a guy. It was a guy at my elementary school, and I couldn't quite comprehend what it was I was feeling. All I knew was that I enjoyed rushing to school at a particular time, to go to a particular place to see a particular guy. We became extremely close friends, nearly inseparable. We would talk every day, play at recess and eat lunch together every day. Those times were great and always well spent, but I wasn't prepared for sixth grade graduation, when I would have to say good-bye to the person who brought me so much excitement. This "feeling" was something I had to explore and try to better understand.

I started finding myself interested in my brother's and cousin's friends who would come by and hang out at the house. I became good at basketball, just so I could play with them and be around them. I would act interested in video games just so I could play with them when they were over. I just enjoyed the thought of being around these guys who were nice to me. I had my crushes, and I enjoyed spending time with them. Though I know now this may not have been a healthy dynamic at the time I felt I needed to explore what it was that made me so excited when they were around.

I would fantasize about seeing their bodies or touching them because I was curious to know what it would be like or what another man's body would look like. I was determined to find out, because there had to be a reason I was so intrigued by the thought of it. I needed to know why. I wanted to see what this was all about, and this became a goal of mine. But how did I approach another guy or initiate an encounter when I had never even explored this before? Would someone get mad at me? Or would someone be accepting and open to exploring this sexuality with me?

Where do I learn how to attain a positive healthy gay relationship? Is it possible? Were there real examples of those relationships? Especially when I was growing up, I only heard negative things pertaining to gay people.

How could I be expected to love and accept myself when it seemed that no one else was accepting of this way of life? It's not like I could turn off how I felt and live a life that society would consider normal. That wasn't me. God makes no mistakes, and I felt assured that He created me the way He did on purpose. He created me to fulfill my purpose. But why did I feel so bad sometimes? Why do I still sometimes second guess whether I think God will be disappointed in me? I have yet to even satisfyingly explore these curiosities and I still feel conflicted. What is this about? Whew! Exploring sex, love and relationships is complicated.

CHAPTER 5
I Am Changing (Love, Sex and Relationships) Love

High school was a whole other world for me. I mean I was starting ninth grade, and it seemed like 30 minutes earlier I was just being born. It seemed the time flew and that I grew up pretty fast. I was actually a year ahead of where I was supposed to be in school because my mom allowed me to start school at the age four. From birth it seems I was a loner. I had nothing to distract my growth milestones. I was talking at like two, maybe even younger, and I was partially reading at the age three. I learned to write at three and a half. I loved to write. So I was ahead of the game when it came to academics but pretty far behind socially in comparison to other ninth graders.

When I first started high school I was very scared. I questioned whether I was smart or attractive enough to fit in. Meeting new people was not an issue because there were so many diverse people from diverse cultures and nationalities at that high school. I felt exposed and revealed to a lost world. It was scary, yet amazing. I really was growing up. Still I was self-conscious because of the rape the previous year. It kinda caused me to shy away from a lot of people. I was "soft" and not like all the other boys walking around trying to act "hard." Weird emotions would constantly surface. The attraction and emotional attachment I had towards other boys grew beyond attraction to a curiosity that I wanted to act on. It was to the point where I couldn't ignore it like I did in the seventh and eighth grades.

High School was so new to me and I felt so lost! As I eagerly sought direction to my third period class after the break which came after second period, I experienced love at first sight! For my very first time I truly felt I was in love after seeing somebody only once. I stood in the middle of the school speechless and in shock! Everything seemed to be going in slow motion like in the movies, and I swear nobody else existed but me and her. Yes, I said her, which only made me even more confused because I had started to believe I only liked guys, but something about her would make anyone re-write all the rules and change the game all together.

The most beautiful girl I've ever seen (well besides my momma and the talented multi-platinum selling, Grammy award winning super star Monica) was only 20 feet away from me! My eyes followed each of her movements! She was a tall, light-skinned, long curly hair, a beautiful body, a wonderful radiant smile, and dreamy eyes. Everything was flawless to me, and this girl could dress. I asked myself, who was this angel? She must've escaped from heaven because I didn't know God created such beautiful people.

That entire day and the days to follow, that sight played over and over again in my mind. There was just something astonishing about her. She was a senior this school year and I was a freshman. Did I have a chance with her? Yeah right! I had already experienced nothing but rejection the majority of my life. There were many who would say I wasn't the finest piece of work in God's woodshop. But at the same time that was my push. I really had nothing to lose.

I admit it was hard for me to muster the strength to go talk to her. She would probably look at me like I was a fool for even existing or breathing her air. After feeling so low, I felt nothing but positive could come from trying. My doubts held me back though. Realistically, how could I step to a senior, one of the popular, most beautiful seniors I had seen at the school, and get her to notice me? I was a "nobody" at this school. And a freshman! Was I insane?

Sure enough I prayed long and hard that night. Isn't it funny how when we feel there is absolutely no other options or choice, we know we can depend on God to help save us or bail us out of our situations. You would of thought I was a deacon the way I was praying this particular night! I prayed for love, happiness, understanding, forgiveness, mercy and I said to God "I don't know if it's meant for me to speak to her. Please spare me the embarrassment. Would you make things different for me this time? I don't think I can bear rejection again! Will you show me a sign or something if it's in your plan for me and her to be introduced? Let me know if this is my imagination or really a significant thing I am supposed to do in my life right now.

Poetry
The Sun and the Clouds
You're my cloud, you're nice and soft.
My cloud floating beyond and off, my cloud forming

many shapes and size, a cloud, incapable of telling
me lies
At times I see images that aren't really there
And you sometimes block my sunshine - you know
that's not fair
Baby-my cloud; you allow me to help you get through
your pain
Expressing it through grey clouds and rain
Baby you're my cloud, you help beautify my sky
You're my cloud-and I'm the sun, this world belongs to
you and I
And as time goes by the sky will eventually be nice
and clear
'Cause we'll be in a whole new world where no one
else can interfere
As your sun, I promise to brighten each and every day
And warm your heart in such a special way,
And when I go 'down' I'll keep your company with the
moon
Letting you know to relax; cause I'll be back soon,
Never too long- I'll always be nice and proud
To be your sunshine if only you'd be my cloud
Her smiles the kind that just brightens up my day
No matter what mood I'm in it affects me in some way
She doesn't know how I feel about her, but it's
obvious that I care
Showing her my tender love proves I'll always be
there
It seems through the rain she could still make my sun
shine
'Cause she's the sweetest person I know, she's one of
a kind
As the days go by I feel my feelings getting stronger
I try to hold it inside but I can't any longer
And when I do try to tell her exactly how I feel

I get the chills and get nervous, and can't let it reveal
She's the girl that I want I swear I'd never need
another
So why won't she tell me what's up with her and I?
Why won't she get wit a brotha?

I know what you are thinking. LOL. Boy you are
too funny, but I was really pouring my heart out in that
poem. I meant every word. The next day during sixth
period I couldn't stop thinking about her. I had a friend
in that class who I told how I felt. He was the only one
who knew. Right as we spoke of her, she walked into
that class.

I was so excited and anxious that I moved crazily
in my seat. Overly-excited I waved at her like there
was no tomorrow, and her being nice, she smiled
back. I then found out she was going to be our
teaching assistant for the remainder of the school
year. I was ecstatic! I also figured out and made
myself believe that this must've been the sign I was
waiting for from God. To me it couldn't be any clearer.
I couldn't help but stare and analyze her. She was so
perfect. I enjoyed each moment so much that I felt
bad the period had to come to an end. That night I
came up with a bright idea. I thought I'd write her a
little letter to better introduce myself. The next day
came and I couldn't wait to see so that I could give
the letter to her and also to see what her response
would be. Could she be my wife to be? I was so
infatuated with her I wanted her to be the mother of
my four kids one day. She was my second dream-
love. She fell in my women-ranking right after Monica!
I have a very vivid imagination and I sometimes live in

a fantasy world built off of the possibility of things.

My friend and classmate motivated me and told me to forget the letters, and go talk to her. But I thought I should do both. It took me ten minutes to get up the nerve to go talk to her. She was sitting in front of the class looking bored. I knew my timing couldn't be any better. So I got up walked slowly towards her, heart pounding, more nervous than ever. It was too late to turn back. I proceeded and actually sat down next to her. More nervous than anything in this world, I began to speak to her.

I erased all of the things I preset in my mind to say and I was just myself and then she looked at me. She got kinda close to me and said,
"Uh... your breath stinks! So please go take your ugly ass right back to your seat and get out of my face. And this letter, you can take this right back because I'm far from interested in what a freshman like you would have to say!" Then she smiled and rolled her eyes. "Naw," she said,
"I was just playing!" She was really a sweetheart and we actually shared a pretty cool short conversation. She told me she appreciated the letter and at the end of class she said good-bye to me.

It's crazy, with something so simple I felt as if at the moment I connected with her my life officially began. It felt like she brought warmth and light to a cold dark world. The kindness and sweetness with which she responded made me like her even more. She was like a breath of fresh air every time I saw her walking around smiling. She was the kind of girl everyone got along with and enjoyed being around.

Only time would tell what this new connection would bring.

Poetry

The Intensity of Your Mind
The capacity of your heart
Leaves me standing here breathless
Not knowing where to start
You're so beautiful
I just can't let my feelings go
I have to speak up
I have to let you know
Baby- tell me exactly
What you feel for me
I'm an understanding person
I will be able to see the things that you are seeing
And why you might feel what you feel
I want you in my life
And I'm keeping it real
So tell me am I what you've been looking for
I have a lot to offer I'll give you much more
Than any other man would
I will fulfill every need believe me I could
But it's your choice tell me if you want me too
If you was to turn me down I don't know what I would do
You'll be missing out
If you turn down a love like mines
If you look in my heart love is what you'll define
And I felt this way for you since the 9th grade
I know a lot of men aren't faithful with me you won't get played
So give me a chance baby and see what I'm about
For some reason I feel you're someone I can't do

without
So that's why I'm trying to win your love
You're an angel of mines sent from above.

The young woman I met in that class that day
was literally the center of my attention. She was all I
could think of and focus on. I have to be honest, I was
tripping! It got to the point where my grades weren't
all that great. I mean here I was in high school, trying
to fit in, trying to act grown, getting in trouble for
stupid things. I had to get it together. Stupid isn't cute!
Why would she want someone who couldn't even
pass a class? I did eventually steer my attention a
little away from her after realizing that she had a
boyfriend whom she'd been with for years. After
seeing him, I didn't blame her one bit for being with
him. He was actually the kinda guy I would wished I
could one day be with.

I found myself attracted to a whole lot of people
for a whole lot of different reasons. Strangely enough
it was both men and women! I was becoming more
comfortable with being bisexual though I may not
have exactly understood what that meant. I was truly
beginning to find myself. I wanted to understand me. I
didn't know that there were so many shallow-minded
people when it came to alternative lifestyles. I was
seeing more and more why people cannot openly be
gay or honest about their sexuality. There was so
much judgment and so many opinions. It was hard to
believe that people are created totally different on
purpose to fulfill their individual purpose, yet some of
us could not be who we truly fully are and we were
expected to live in limitation. What kind of life is that?
If this is what's expected, then who could ever be

happy with themselves. This was all new to me so I didn't want to chance losing the few new friends I was making, but I surely found myself expressing my interest in different individuals at individual times. It wasn't always easy though, because each expression was like a gamble, or rolling dice. I never knew if I would crap out and have the entire school know my business, or if I'd get a good roll and another chance at it. It's like I had to face different levels and possibilities of rejection. It became such a constant thing that I realized I had to develop skin much tougher than the average person and even tougher than what I had already developed. It didn't help I was awkward looking and had to deal with my own conflicting sexuality/lifestyle. It was all so hard for me to understand. How could I expect someone else to embrace and accept me? It was difficult living a life that was kinda in secret yet was simply a part of who I was and had always been. I was just finally learning to live in my truth, but how was I supposed to accept or embrace myself when every indication stated that I was a mistake or something to be ashamed of?

To be honest, that's what kept me in the closet. I realized the non-acceptance because there was a popular senior guy, who was actually my girl crushes' best-friend, who was suspected of being gay. His reputation went down the drain because of the suspicion. It was so crazy seeing the torment that he went through and how he had to deal with the scrutiny of his peers and classmates. However, his best friend was a very sweet, loving, and a caring person and I'm sure she would've been accepting of his sexual preference but I believe it was a secret he had to keep to himself. I felt bad for him, knowing his fear of losing her or changing the dynamics of their friendship, but I felt great about the fact that I still was getting to know her more and more throughout the year and we were developing an actual friendship.

I seemed to write her letters every single day. I just had so much to say. I'm not even sure if she read them all. I wrote her so often she didn't even have the opportunity to respond. I'm not even sure if my letters were interesting, but she was so kind that she would simply accept them and thank me for the thought and consideration.

I found myself to be very interested in the outcome of the situation with her best friend. I kinda looked at this situation as indication for me to know what would happen if people found out about my curiosities. I related to him but I never was aware of how hard it would be to deal with the exposure of such a lifestyle. He was a very attractive dark-skinned fella, so he had his way with many of the girls at the high school which made it all harsher for him after being exposed. All these ladies faced embarrassment and tried to put him down even more to defend themselves and to save their own embarrassment. I respected him so much because I would never see him sweat. He was a soldier. He chilled mainly by himself when he wasn't around his best girlfriend.

As time went on, I realized how slim my chances were with my girl crush and I began to find myself attracted to him as well. Yes, he was attractive and had something appealing about him but I don't think it was just his looks or personality, I really think it was just because he was said to be gay. I figured it would be easy to fulfill my curiosities with him. This was the year I considered myself to be in the experimental stage of my life. I finally started liking myself, and after building a friendship with my girl crush, I began gaining a lot more confidence. Monica's music also helped me with my self-esteem and pride. I began looking into the mirror and finding it easier to recognize things that were worthwhile about me, things that I could value. These were great times for me to start believing in me.

Poetry

Sensual Kisses

Using sensual kisses without any words, your love makes me feel higher than a sky full of birds.
My heart pounds rapidly with every thought of you, I feel so much passion, I no longer knew what to do.
I tried to keep my composure and withhold how I felt, but with every word you speak I'm assured my love is real.
Regardless of society, I can't care less about what's considered right I'm living for a love that seems to shine so bright.
Brighter than the sun on a summer day, your sexy ass smile blows my mind away.
The way fantasies unfold with one look into your eyes, they lead my heart to love and my heart never lies.
I trust you with my life, you mean everything to me.
When I needed guidance you took me under your wing.
I don't live by others expectations I live for a continuous smile, one that didn't come 'til I met you.
And now I've been happy for a while.
With the titles we're given love flows through the

blood and veins taking chances with your heart brings much happiness and some pain.
I collected my thoughts after feeling so much sorrow you came in my life and promised a better tomorrow.
You can call me selfish and say I'm naive, I just want to love you I have no tricks up my sleeve.
I know it's kind of a bad position that I have put you in, but that's only if you live to please others otherwise let our good times begin.
I as your love will be very understanding, you could handle your business, I'm not too demanding.
Just at many times I'll want you to hold behind the closing of our door,
And I'll show you that I love you rather than telling you like before.
No pressures and no regrets, I've fallen with no safety-nets, this love I feel is eternal and free,
And nobody can give it to you because nobody's like me.

As I started building my confidence, I really wanted to work on the way I looked. It had to start with the clothes. Then I took it to the hair. Then my face! I still spent most weekends alone because I hadn't many friends. Once in high school, the one question I heard as often as my name was "What is it you are striving to be or do professionally?" Shit, I don't know! I'm trying to figure out who I am first, before I decide what "I" want to do. Honestly, I was unsure of what I wanted to do career-wise. But I figured the answers would come, I just had to learn to ask the right questions.

I first considered being a counselor but I had too

many problems of my own. I wanted to be a teacher or a lawyer but I didn't like school all that much. I even thought about going into the Air Force but I got kicked out of my ROTC class. It was a difficult year. As time went by, I made more and more friends. I was much more sociable and people seemed to like me. I felt at this point that high school was going to be the best years of my life. On weekends I'd find myself walking to the park, or to the local Wal-Mart (to keep up with Monica in all the latest magazines) or even to the mall. I was used to being alone but it didn't necessarily make me happy. I was this way since I was a kid. Of course I wanted friends, or someone to always come visit me but for some reason that I still don't understand my friends never really seemed welcome over my house. I wasn't ever allowed to have my friends spend the night or chill until late at night except for a boy who lived down the street. He was over at our house so much he was like another brother of ours. My older brother seemed to be allowed to have his friends over. I don't know if it was because he was older, or if it was that my parents assumed the fate of my sexuality. It made no sense to me. It kinda limited me to getting close with friends because I wouldn't feel comfortable not being able to go to their house to chill or them not being welcome where I lived. It kinda took the enjoyment out of it.

I began to affiliate myself with more of my brother's friends because they were always at our house. It didn't really help me much because in time I started finding them attractive. It's not that my mother was really strict, but it was that she and my dad had to agree on everything, and it seems whenever it came to me or my life a disagreement was in order. I can honestly say that ever since they were married, for the most part I never really felt equal to my brother with regard to the respect, understanding, responsibility, and privileges they gave to him. I always felt like the fifth wheel. I was just simply in the way all the time. There were many times I felt I wasn't loved. It was more like I was just being tolerated. This really is something I took into account when it came to me deciding if or how I would tell my parents that I liked guys.

For some reason I have felt that way for the majority of all my life. I began building up animosity and disdain toward my family and didn't really feel as if I fit in with them. Maybe it was all in my mind, but it seemed to be true during this period in my life more than ever. I would get in trouble for the little things at home constantly. For the big things, I received understandable punishment. I always felt like I was a failure and as if I couldn't do anything right no matter how hard I tried. I was always being yelled at and that made me timid with everything I did. I couldn't think clearly many times because I was intimidated and thought I would get yelled at or in trouble. I tried hard to do right and to make my mother and dad proud of me but most times when I did things right, it was like nothing ever happened. No acknowledgement, no words, no thoughts, nothing at all. At least that's how it felt.

Usually I received no type of encouragement or recognition, only when I was wrong. I so badly wanted to please them. I began lying to them about everything just to get them to like me a little more, even when I wasn't in the wrong or had no logic or reason behind the lie. I wanted to say the right things, do the right things, and be the right thing. There was no pleasing the displeased. Being a kid, feeling unloved or as misunderstood wasn't a healthy situation for me. It was another factor that initiated the depression I couldn't shake for a while. It also triggered another stage of feeling suicidal, and it was all due to feeling unwanted, unloved, unappreciated.

I never felt good about coming home from school cause I knew there was always going to be something I would get yelled at about and the same routine started to get kind of old. The smallest things would bring some of the biggest confrontations down on me. When I felt something was unfair, I would talk to my mom about it and most times she would just say, "It's only because your dad wants you to be more responsible! Think before you do stuff!" So here I am thinking "should even express these feelings and curiosities I am having?"

I wanted to be able to ask questions that I wouldn't be judged for asking. Who should I talk to about this stuff? I found myself always creating things to do just so I could get out of the house. I would go to friend's houses that weren't really my friends, but a way for me to not have to feel trapped in a home in which I wasn't wanted. I always felt invisible or as if I didn't exist. I was over looked and irrelevant. I was already confused enough about how I felt, and now I questioned the purpose of my existence. This is something I began growing accustomed to.

I figured it was always going to be this way so I had to live with it. It was going to be just me against the world. After that I tried to remain "active" or "busy" so I wouldn't have to be home too much to avoid making more mistakes or getting my parents mad at me. One Saturday I felt my dad's energy was a little off, so I wanted to do whatever it took to get out the house and stay out of the way. I decided I would get dressed and walk to Wal-Mart and to the mall after that. I felt very confident in my looks today! I had on some of my favorite blue-jeans, some new mustard Sketcher boots, and my cousin's Bengal Jersey. I must admit that it was an interesting experience walking to the mall.

During long walks, I would always sing Monica songs, from each one on her first album to any other she was featured on. It made my walks peaceful ones. In the middle of my ninth song — *Before You Walk Out of My Life*[2] — I noticed a green Cavalier on the other side of the street. It seemed to be following me. I was by a McDonald's about to approach a stoplight. The car went to the light and made a U-Turn. I began to panic. I was not in the mood to deal with some craziness today and all I could think of was flashbacks of what had happened to me before.

My heart started pounding. I started walking faster. The driver hurried up to park in the McDonald's parking lot I was soon going to approach. This guy got out of his car and then went to the pay-phone that was near the path I was on. As I passed by mad-

---

[2] *Before You Walk Out of My Life* - writer(s): Kenneth Karlin, Carsten Schack, Andrea Monica Martin. Copyright: Soulvang Music, EMI Blackwood Music Inc., Full Of Soul Music, Sailandra Publishing, Almo Music Corp, 1995.

dogging (I figured if he tried something I was going to know what his ass looked like!) I was almost completely past him before he asked, "Do you know what time it is?" I firmly said, "No!" and I kept walking.

I was going to the mall but the whole situation scared me and I suddenly wished I was home. I was on my way, and then the same car pulled up next to me and there were two guys in the car. Oh my God, not this again. I saw them look at me as I picked up a brick and readied my position to throw it. The driver talked trying to be cool, but I was ready to fight. I was in self-defense mode. I held the brick in my hand the whole time we talked. I still felt stupid for even talking with them.

He began asking me questions. "What's your name? What school do you go to? Do you know so and so? How about him? Where do you live?"

I answered most of the questions with questions. Nothing specific. Then he said, "I'm new out here in Palmdale, and don't really know my way around so maybe we could kick it sometime and you could show me around." I realized this guy was probably harmless. I replied "Okay." and accepted his phone number.

I called him that night and we talked. We also talked for the three nights that followed. I asked him if he was gay and told him I was basically what they called "bi-curious." He told me he wanted to be my man and that he'd show me the "ropes." I wasn't having luck with the ladies so I was with it.

This boy told me he was 18 years old, and that he went to Palmdale High school. Everything but his name and number turned out to be lies. He was really out of school and he was about 21 or 22. I had just turned 15. Most people would say that I was mature for my age and that I passed for being older than I was. But before I learned the truth about him, we kicked it for like three months, "going together" or whatever it would be called. He fucked up when he tried to pressure me into having sex. I lost interest real quick. He introduced me to his two closest friends with whom I ended up becoming great friends. One was the one in the car with him the day they drove up to me. In reality, I was far from attracted to him, and I figured if I wanted to experiment, I could. I also enjoyed the idea of being able to ask all the questions I had about this lifestyle that I couldn't ask anyone else.

He was just the first opportunity I had. I did a few (very few) sexual things with him. Most of it kinda felt forced because I just wasn't feeling it. I was glad the two friends respected me and they told me the truth about everything because they said they didn't want me to get into anything that messy. They kept it real with me from the beginning and I love them for it.

This guy had some serious issues! He was frequently trying to use or take advantage of the young kids who didn't know any better! When I left him, he tried so hard to get back with me because I was the only one he couldn't have his way with. I definitely remained cool with my two new friends though. I wanted to leave him completely, but was just trying to find the right way. Then my mother decided one day that she wanted to go through my personal stuff and found some letters from him. She asked me about them but my whole attitude was if she hadn't gone through my stuff she wouldn't have found something she didn't want to see. The letters were very expressive and I am sure she read some stuff she did not want to read. When she demanded I never see him again I felt it was not her place to choose my friends for me. While my initial intentions were to stop seeing him anyway I remained in touch only to rebel from my mom because she wasn't being fair or logical in my eyes!

Although my experience was a bad example, I knew was at a point where I wanted more experiences. Whenever I was at school, I found myself wanting and lusting after my female crush's best friend. It would be a challenge but I wanted to take it on before I realized it would mess up my chances with my female crush (as if I had a chance). Because of that I left it alone.

This was a good high school year for me because a lot of good went down. I had a lot of new experiences. Near the end of this year I met a guy who was kinda popular and a star football player at my high school. He was real cool and someone I had an instant connection with. It just felt like we would be close friends right away. We met because during lunch time, we just happened to occasionally kick it with the same two girls. One of the two girls was like a sister to him, so they were always around one another. We began a mild friendship after being around each other so often. This was surely a blossoming friendship.

The end of the year was fast approaching and it was about to be Christmas break. I just had to get my crush a gift. Lord knows I was broke. I ended up getting her a teddy bear, a card, and I think, some fake Bath and Body Works lotion my mother didn't want. I don't remember exactly but I do know it was heart-felt. It didn't cost anything either. The teddy bear I got off of my little brother's bed. My mom was about to throw them away anyway, the other stuff was stuff my mom didn't want. It was on! I couldn't wait to see my crushes reaction either. And I remember I gave her an old dried out rose too. It was pretty. My mom used to hang them up-side down as they died then sprayed them with gloss, and it becomes a beautiful decoration, and I gave her one that was orange and yellow, with a poem and a letter. She appreciated the gifts. In her mind she might have thought "how cheap" but she had to admit that the gifts were totally unique. She truly seemed appreciative and was excited that I was so thoughtful and that I did this for her. I am grateful for those truly happy and unforgettable memories.

Right before graduation at our school, they held a celebration called May Fest! It was the bomb! All kinds of different foods, music, and games. Lunch lasted for an hour and a half on this particular day of the school year. But this was the day I had to face a harsh reality. The reality was that my crush had a boyfriend and she was happy with him. I had to agree that he was a dime. I could see exactly why she was with him and I was jealous of both of them for having the other. Up until that day I was wondering who had won the heart of my special woman. At this point I gave up trying to win her love but I couldn't stop writing her letters, they had become routine. I felt like she was the only one who made time to hear me express myself and to be who I was. I felt we had a special type of connection. I felt we had an understanding. It meant the world to me.

Poetry

What if I Could Make You Love Me as Much as I Love You?
What if I could tell you things that'll stay between me and you?
What if we could be together when every day becomes new?
What if we would kiss every day when we see each other at school?
What if I asked you out and you said "yes,"
That feeling in my heart would be the best,
Because you are the only one I need,
Let's stay together to see where this relationship will lead,
What if we get married and buy a place to live,
We'll be together forever-much love we will give,
Then one day we will have a child,
We will spank his ass if he starts acting wild,
What if we're still together when we're old and our hairs are grey?
And your passion still burned by the sweet things I would say,
We'll live to see our grand kids go on their first date,
And we'll be taking pictures when they graduate,
What if we died and were buried with each other,
So for the rest of our "after-lives" we'll lay with one another,

And our kids and their kids will look to us, they'll
admire our love for each other and our built up trust,
What if these things really came true?
It'll be the best thing to that happened to you,
because I'll treat you like a beautiful queen,
I know what I know- you know what I mean?
Days passed.
On my walks home from school when I would miss
the bus (which was like an hour walk)
I was thinking of my crush and wondering what she
thought of me.
I didn't know if I was annoying to her, if she
appreciated my letters, if I was in over my head.
I was wondering would she tell me if she got tired of
them.
So many questions, and they kept running through my
head.
I thought, "I want you but I don't 'cause I just wanna
be your friend and I want you to know that I like you
but what message should I send?"
I felt so much attraction since the day our eyes met,
We've shared plenty of conversations and never did
you fret,
Because you are a person that is sweet at heart,
And I think it's time for a closer relationship between
us to start,
So what should I do to create a chance with you?
Because when you're around there are so many
things I wanna do,
Only God will know
And the love I'll show will help determine how far up
our relationship will grow,
I just wanna pull you near and say "you're mines"
Who knows true love is what we might find,
So tell me are you willing to see if things will work out,

I'll satisfy all your needs and for that there will be no doubt.

I kept on singing Monica's *Why I Love You So Much*[3] and then realized my crush was about to graduate and be gone. This made me kind of emotional. So I began singing *Before You Walk Out Of My Life*[4]. I know this all sounds crazy, but this was really my peace of mind. This is how I killed time and stayed in a positive mindset.

One day I was 20 minutes away from home and my crush passed by in a car with her brother. I saw her but didn't think she saw me so I continued with my song. Two words later, I noticed her car turning around! She did see me! She and her brother stopped and asked me if I needed a ride home. I was nervous but grateful at the same time. They gave me a ride home and of course I was very thankful and felt special that she would stop for little ol' me. I felt as good as I would if Monica were to pull me on stage at one of her concerts or something.

I appreciated and cherished that moment and I still do. It obviously meant she cared somewhat for me. She cared enough to turn around. I know other people would keep rolling and tell me the next day that they saw me. The end of the school year was getting closer and closer. For many bad reasons, it

---

[3] *Why I Love You So Much* - writer: Daryl Simmons. Copyright: Boobie And DJ Songs Inc., Warner-Tamerlane Publishing Corp., 1995.

[4] *Before You Walk Out Of My Life* - writer(s): Kenneth Karlin, Carsten Schack, Andrea Monica Martin. Copyright: Soulvang Music, EMI Blackwood Music Inc., Full Of Soul Music, Sailandra Publishing, Almo Music Corp., 1995.

seemed her relationship with her best friend was on the rocks. It seemed like the last few months were like hell for him and she wasn't really hanging with him as much as she used to. I really felt bad for him.

I wondered where he could get so much strength to deal with all the drama for so long. I guess he had no choice but to be as strong as he was. Because of the strength he exhibited I gained a lot more respect and admiration toward him. I wanted to get to know him and I mean all of him. I wanted to tell him but how was I supposed to do that? So I didn't do anything. But after he graduated we had the opportunity to speak and he told me everything. We never hooked up because he moved out of state. Before the end of that year, I knew I had to give my crush my all my heart to make sure she'd never forget me, so she would remember me always and forever.

Poetry

I Give My All To You
I'm smiling
Because of your last spoken word
It's far more passionate
Than all that I've ever heard
Captivated
You came and swept me off my feet
Only by your personality
And how I felt when our eyes would meet
Not knowing you from Adam,
Norman, or Steve,
Could this be my angel?
Some may not believe
But I know that finally

God saw my love straight through
And allowed it to appear
When directed towards you
I may be dreaming
But I wouldn't be awake
I'm falling for you baby
And it isn't a mistake
Every other thought that invades
Pertains to you
It's driving me crazy
I don't know what to do
All the people that would approach
Are playing a game with no 'ball'
All I want is you
I'm giving you my all!

I thought of the end of that school year as possibly the very last time I would see her or maybe even the last opportunity for me to express myself to her if there were any words I hadn't said. I actually wrote her a 49 page letter front and back of each page. Yes, I did and it took me a week to write it. I told her in the letter almost everything about me -- how she made me feel and how I hoped to remain her friend throughout our lives. It was like a mini book. It was the longest letter I had ever written. It was so many papers, I had to roll it up and put a rubber-band around it.

Don't Search for Love
Because sometimes you just won't see
All things in store for you
Wait for destiny
I'm always going to be here
Whether you need a friend or much more

If you need someone to talk to
You'll always have access to my door.
I not only admire you for your personality
But you're one of a kind
Not like all others
That's why I wish you were mines
As long as I have your friendship
I feel quite secure
Because I'll always be true to you
To keep our friendship pure
If you feel lonely at night
Just pick up the phone
I'll see to it
That you never feel alone
If you never reach out to me
How could you ever expect me to touch?
The angel that I found in you
And admire so much.

I was seriously infatuated with her. Now when I
think about it that letter was a bit much, but literally
wrote this girl a letter almost every single day, even on
some of my lonely weekends. I can hardly imagine
now how many letters she had from me. I often
wondered if she kept them. I didn't understand my
strong attraction or feelings for her. I assumed it to be
love 'cause how else would one define the butterflies
she would give me every time I saw her? She didn't
write back but I think I never really allowed her the
opportunity to. She'd respond in person most times.

Poetry

I Think I Love You!
It took some time-but only time could tell,
I'm really feelin' you and I know you pretty well,
It all seems weird because I don't want anyone but you,
Every time you come to mind smile is all I can do;
When you come around I still get butterflies inside,
You give me confidence and a sense of pride,
When I'm low you find a way to bring me high,
And my heart beats fast whenever we touch I don't even know why,
I'd do anything for you including making a sacrifice,
It's all because you're such a big part of my life,
When we had sex it felt special to an extent,
I knew it wasn't a temporary thing but that it was meant,
I would never cheat or hurt you it's not a part of my plan,
I want you to be happy I wanna remain your man,
At 1st I had doubts wondering if this is true,
But baby it has to because I think I love you.

By now it was the very end of the year, after graduation and the day of the senior trip. All I could remember was the feeling of love I felt whenever she was around or came to mind. I began to feel sad and depressed. It would be my last day to see her. I literally tried waiting around for their bus to arrive back at the school because I wanted my chance to say goodbye. I also had a time I needed to be home, and I didn't know how long it would take for them to get back.

They got back from their senior trip about 3:30 but I had already begun walking home. I was about 15 minutes into my walk and something made me turn around only to see that their buses were arriving back at the school from their senior trip. I ran as fast as I could (like Forrest Gump) all the way back to where the buses parked and when I approached, she was getting off the bus. I was all out of breath, slightly sweating, and I said to her, "I just wanted to say goodbye!" She said, "Don't say goodbye, goodbye means forever. Let's just say adios." Then she smiled, gave me a letter, and a hug.

That moment meant so much to me and I will never forget the feeling I had inside at that moment. It was one of the best moments of my life. My crush actually wrote me back and gave me a hug! She made me feel as if it were important for her to see me again one day.

Poetry

My Heart Skipped a Beat Today
Because you touched me in a special way,
It really did catch me off guard,
If you would've touched me in some places you would've felt something hard,
It seems I've been one to notice you from afar,
Only to recognize how beautiful you are,
Never did I imagine coming across someone like you,
You're constantly on my mind-what am I supposed to do?
People like you-I only see in my dreams,
But it's not a dream-so are you really all that you seem?

Maybe you're just another fantasy
But if you aren't-would you mind being with me?
I want to get to know you in a much better way,
Maybe we'll fall in love and get married one day!

I cried tears of happiness and sighs of love as I read her letter repeatedly while walking home. My heart felt so warm. It was a feeling I would never be able to understand with words. An unexplainable feeling. A day to be cherished for eternity. I still read that letter every now and then for encouragement. I didn't get the girl in the end but I did get something with much more value I got her friendship. I couldn't have been more satisfied.

Poetry

Tenderness In You
There is tenderness in you that I've never seen before,
Your sexiness is radiant causing mouths to hit the floor,
I admire you from a distance-noticing good qualities from afar,
Which makes it all more interesting getting to know who you are?
Your smiles like a rainbow-full of light and very bright,
Your beauty goes far beyond what I see in sight,
Your personality is addicting
I love to just be around,
Thanking god every day for blessing me with this angel that I've found,
Your friendship I'll always cherish you're honest and very true,
That could be another reason I'm falling for you!

I get butterflies inside whenever you're in reach,
My words can't even flow right because you make me
blur my speech,
I dreamed of this day to come face to face with you,
Now that my dream came true I don't know what to
do,
I wanna grab you by your hand and bring your body
near,
I wanna be there for everything-I wanna wipe each
tear.
I wanna be the one you go to when there's something
on your mind,
I wanna show you that I'm the truest love that you'll
ever find!
Our conversations are intriguing your heart is very
pure,
This is something I wanna pursue I'd never been so
sure,
I wouldn't depend on this for happiness you may be
one to disappoint,
Though I can guarantee you'd get high off my love no
need to smoke a joint,
The only way we'll know if this is meant to be,
Is taking the chance- and that's how we'll see!
What are your chances of this all shining through?
Well, I don't know-it all depends on you,
Are you serious or only half way,
If you're not interested then it's okay
You need to let me know something whether it be
good or bad,
For true friendship is at least what I'm hoping we'd
have.

This freshman year of high school definitely
ended on a good note, something for me to really

smile about. If this was high school I want to stay there forever. But now it was the summer. I didn't do anything spectacular like always. I was definitely eager to see what the tenth grade would have in store for me.

Poetry

You
If I found somebody new to complete my world,
The day I see them my mind would become UN-twirled,
Because you would've answered a lot of my deepest concerns,
Like "will my passion in my heart ever start to burn?"
And it did the first day we met; I'm finally happy and always will be I bet
As long as I have You.
Now I have a smile on my face and it won't go away, I hope You don't decide to go-so what should I say?
I would want to say I love You but it would be too soon,
You would be the one on my mind when I look up at the stars and the moon
I would have this weird feeling that remains in my heart,
And if You leave my side You would tear it all apart,
So if I tell You I love You even though I don't know if it's true,
Please understand I don't want anybody but You
When I get lonely I can just call on You,
Good thing You're there otherwise I wouldn't know what to do,
You should know you've won a spot in my heart,
Your personality is bomb, You look good and You're

smart
Nobody can compare to You
You're the one I've been searching for my whole life
through,
And now that I've found You I don't know what to do,
Maybe kiss You, squeeze You, and hold You tight,
And we would sit up and talk all night,
But this can't happen if You're not here,
So it's time I stop dreaming' and You appear,
I'm tired of living a fantasy,
Thinking I'm in love and finally happy,
But who knows if it'll happen, if my days in reality
remain blue,
Make a dream come true, hey! I'm talking to You.

Love. It's strange how with the passing of time
and with the different experiences I've had my
perception of love has changed. I used to value love
as one of the best things in the world. Something that
each person should strive to attain with extra effort. I
guess I was right to an extent. Love could be a very
beautiful thing. An amazing, unexplainable
experience, but in the same sense it can ruin your life.

I will say that in my life, each of my encounters
with love has been extremely different from the other.
Some of the times were extremely good and others
broke my heart while others simply weren't real.
Sometimes I would misconstrue the emotional
attachment that sex sometimes brought and confuse
it with love. Other times I never wanted to experience
love again. So if you ask me now what my perception
of love is I can't say I have a standing perception. I
just tend to have quite a few opinions about it.

Poetry

Do I want Love?
Of course!
Do I long to be loved? Definitely.
Do I have Love-not quite?
Do I still have faith in Love? I don't know.
What does Love mean to you?

I find myself most content loving myself now because with that love I know it's real. I know what I'm getting, and I know what to expect. I know I'll never let myself down nor will I ever lie or cheat myself in any way. I learned to love myself continuously in all the ways others seem incapable. Only I know the type of loving I need. I know what makes me happy. Beyoncé couldn't have said it better when she said, "Just me and I it's all I got in the end, that's what I found out." And it's the truth, I'm all I have.

At spontaneous times like now, I find myself a little uneasy and partially depressed. I don't understand my emotions like I used to. I mean at times I feel on top of the world and then at other times I want that world to end. I find myself feeling lonely yet at the same time I want to be alone. I feel so alone in this world as if no one will ever be able to understand me fully, yet I feel no one even cares to try. I guess I started not to care for anyone to try. I don't want too many people in my life. I've even let go of a few old friends because they weren't living up to their end of the friendship. It may sound a little arrogant but in life, you have to know what you want in order to eventually be satisfied.

In friendships I expect loyalty, truth, honesty, love, sincerity and to simply be a friend. I don't feel it's too much to ask. But is it? I mean, there's got to be a reason no one new seems to live up to my expectations. I could say I'm happy too but at the same time, I'm not in many respects. That's why I said I don't know how to explain my emotions anymore. They are all new to me. Love is a very touchy subject. It is very fragile to me and though I've given it a few attempts, I have had very few others who loved me back. I sometimes look at the ocean and realize how endless it appears to be. Well, that's how my love is. Endless, constant, deep, refreshing and much more than I can even imagine.

The hardest thing is learning to differentiate when I like, but not love someone. Because I imagine possibilities or because of the connection I feel, it's crazy. There are times when I've really liked a person but I said, "You're well-made but you weren't made for me. You may be a lot of what I asked for but you are not in the packaging God intended for me. I can't help but want to open you up and claim you as my own, but you're not meant for me, you simply aren't for me."

Is love love when you grow accustomed to loving someone more than the love you provide for yourself? How could that be? Maybe I'm dependent on the love given to help determine the love I feel I deserve, especially when it's been so long since I've really had it in my reach or grasp. I know I love myself but I still hold so many doubts and insecurities that I sometimes long to be held, and loved, and appreciated.

Being lonely is real. So is love. Love is real when it comes from a real source. There are many actors out there so I had to learn how to tell when someone was the real deal and when they were not. The hardest part was facing reality when it was revealed. It's not always what I hoped it would be or what it appeared to be. I found the feeling of not feeling worthy enough to be loved the way I dreamed to be very painful. Because of circumstances I allowed and promoted others' happiness before my own. I felt I wasn't worthy of reciprocated feelings and appreciation, at least not to the same degree I gave to them. I came to find out that I couldn't seek love from another person in order to classify or justify whether I was deserving of love.

The way I truly began to reestablish my self-worth was through self-love. That began when I stopped allowing people to step on me and diminish my worth. I realized when I was selling myself short and when I was not living up to my full potential. God shows us daily that He loves us and it takes our love for ourselves in order for us to see it, embrace it and appreciate it. Why is it that we put in so much energy into receiving love from someone else when we already have the greatest God's love?

Most would say we want to feel as if we have a tangible love -- one that can be touched and felt physically -- but all things tangible will disappear in time. Why is everlasting, eternal love not enough? At least it doesn't appear to be! Naturally we long for connection and that's how a lot of emotional and human feeling is justified or defined in our lives.

Poetry

You're Not as Good as You Used to Look
I remember when I first saw you
I was speechless and in awe
You had to be the flyest king
Sexiest being I ever saw
In twenty minutes
2,000 fantasies explored in my mind and all I could think was
You had to be one of a kind?
So I played the co-star
As you made a mockery of my life's movie
The ways you penetrated
And sent chills and grooves through me
Had me on cloud nine
Even when it was a cloudless sky
The attraction-one sided I just couldn't deny
Must have been poetic
The ways you said the right things at the right times
I'm not even into sex like that
But truly you blew my mind
So much put into something
That just wanted to put out
Had me standing lonely in my own shadows
Wondering what it was about
So hurt, so dumb, I allowed myself to be deceived
You said you liked me, that I was cool,
Why was I so quick to believe?
'Cause after our hours, our minutes, and our seconds of sex

It was even more apparent that you couldn't care less
It took me months to move on
I gave you so many things I wanted back
Now you're not as good as you used to look
Because I know within-you're whack
It doesn't help that I learned
After allowing myself to fail
Though I get flashbacks when I see you
I still proceed to tell you go to hell
Love what the hell do you want from me?
So many times I felt like a victim,
You allowed me to be deceived
You're not all you're made out to be
Why was I so quick to believe?
All the people that's supposed to represent you
Seems as if they were sent to demolish my heart and
make me resent you
I tend to give you chance after chance
To find myself disappointed despite the circumstances
All I gotta ask you Love-What the hell you want from
me?
I gave you my heart
So much of my time
I allowed you control over my spirit and mind
In the end I just find myself back where I began
Love you're something I'll never fully understand
Are you for me? If not why do you accept as I return?
If you're supposed to ignite all passion why do I
always burn?
When will I learn?
Makes me wonder if I should let go love
What the hell you want from me
'Cause I surely don't know
I can't believe in you the same
Because you never come through

So Love
I now realize
I don't want shit from you
But Love, what the hell you want from me?

CHAPTER 6
The Cocoon

In a book I love called *Mr. Dream Merchant*[5]
there is a part where the author speaks about the "Gift
in the Struggle." He begins by telling about a little boy
who was playing one day and as he approached a
tree, he saw a butterfly fighting to break free from its
cocoon. As he watched in excitement and
anxiousness he began to feel bad for the butterfly
because no matter how hard it was fighting and trying
to break through, it didn't seem to be working. The
little boy decided that he was going to help, so he
opened up the hole a little knowing that with his
assistance the butterfly would be able to break free.
He was right. The butterfly broke free and as it began
to flutter its wings to fly free it fell to the ground and
began walking as the caterpillar it once was. The little
boy was confused! He even took to picking it up and
throwing it in the air thinking it would boost the
butterfly's ability to fly, but it was to no avail.

The next day, the little boy went to school and
he couldn't concentrate. The boy explained to his
teacher what happened with the butterfly hoping for
an explanation because he couldn't understand why if
something was free why wouldn't it soar. The teacher
explained to him that sometimes when something is
expected to endure and handle something before it's
time it may not be equipped to do so. The teacher
mentioned the fact that the time, struggle and effort
that it takes for a butterfly to be freed from its cocoon

---

[5] *Mr. Dream Merchant* by Erroll J. Bailey, Element Books Ltd; May 1998.

allows it to build the strength required in to fly. If it's freed too soon, it hasn't developed enough stamina to handle the next level or stage of its life, and it will resort back to what it knows and what it's used to, in this case walking like a caterpillar even though it has wings. The teacher told the little boy that not all struggle is meant for suffering, most times it's meant to help us learn and become stronger from it so we can endure what's to come in life as we get closer to our purpose. The teacher reiterated that by him helping the butterfly get out, it may no longer be strong enough to realize its full potential unless it endures something else that will allow it to gain the strength it needed. The little boy thought about this and thought his teacher's explanation made complete sense.

A week later, the little boy came across another tree with a butterfly trying to break free of its cocoon, and this time the little boy watched, and said, "Don't worry little butterfly, you'll be free soon, and you will be free and you'll be much happier. Just push through this." Moments later when the butterfly broke free, it fluttered its wings and it was able to fly! The butterfly flew around the boy's head a few times as if it was thanking him for allowing the struggle. I look at that fable as a testament to how I can live my life. I am comforted by the fact that I will be able to make it through if I can just endure some of the hardships life throws at me and learn from them. There truly is a gift in my struggle.

At times I feel like a butterfly and that a part of my purpose is to fly and soar free, but there are also some things that confine me to just walking. I am fighting through these things, but I can see glimpses of the possibilities. I'm tryna break through my cocoon but I haven't yet gained the strength I need, so it seems as if the struggle gets longer and longer, harder and harder, and the more strength I seem to be gaining. It makes me feel as if my ability to continue to fight is draining away. People are looking at me telling me it'll be okay one day, but I am starting to believe that is just something they were trained to say. Did they go through this? Did they have to struggle like I am struggling? Most times I think "no" so how are they gonna tell me that the outcome of my struggling will be good or promising? How can they even be close when they have never had to endure what I am enduring? I know my purpose is to be greater than a mere caterpillar, although there's nothing wrong with being a caterpillar, but that's not the life meant for me. I know was created to soar and fly free.

I'm starting to believe that struggling is a constant thing 'cause once I broke through the cocoon and began soaring, but I soon came to stop. I had to struggle a bit more. To me this transition into a butterfly is my purpose. Maybe there's another cocoon I am meant to break through. Who knows what I will become once I break through the next layer and the next cocoon. And just how many layers are there? How much more struggle? Does it ever end? Will I consistently be striving to evolve into something greater for the remainder of my existence on earth? Are these even cocoons?

Wouldn't life be so much easier if it came with a manual? That's probably impossible. I mean, who could ever predict or foresee all that a person will endure in life? Every person's life is designed totally differently, so how would one manual be able to capture all of the possibilities of all the different paths? I think of the many different things I have overcome or conquered. There was a gift in each struggle. I gained some knowledge, wisdom, understanding, awareness or lessons from each struggle. Most of the situations also shaped and formed me into the person I was created to be. When I was going through each thing it was important that instead of complaining about it, I sought the message, lesson or wisdom meant to be gained from the situation. Some of those times were the most random things that could occur, and the lesson was to never do that it again and I just had to laugh.

Life is not easy, and so many people give up because of the different circumstances that they have had to endure. The cards that were dealt may have been too hard for some to play. The hardest thing for me was the lack of support, understanding and resources so that I was just left to try to figure things out for myself.

I am sharing my story because there truly is life after tragedy, hardship, pain, and heartache. There truly is a gift in the struggle. Nothing I went through was in vain. There's no manual to life, but I hope that by sharing a part of my journey and the ways that I dealt with my struggles will give someone else the courage or strength to keep fighting. What works for me may not work for everyone but at least one person is giving you his perspective. Life is ten percent of what happens to us and 90 percent of how we react to what happens.

CHAPTER 7
Faith

When I think of struggle, I can't help but think about another one of the most defining moments in my life. I remember I was working at the Virgin Megastore in Burbank, and I had a green Mitsubishi Mirage. At this time in my life, I was truly in transition. There's a gift in the struggle right? Well, the struggle got really real.

I wasn't necessarily welcome to live at home because I didn't quite seem to see eye to eye with my dad at the time. I was fresh out of a program in which I had been living and was looking for my own place to live. It very well may have been my age, I was now 19 but I truly was trying to get myself together and become more responsible. When I say transition, I really mean transition. I was living with a friend of mine, and at the time I was doing pretty good at my job at Virgin Megastore and I was actually getting a second job that was only a summer gig at the Old Navy at the Northridge Mall. I remember how complicated things were at this time because I didn't make a lot of money at all, and my hours were very limited but I was determined to keep up with my car note and to pay the amount I needed to stay in the room I was renting from my friend. I felt like things were coming together in my life, and I was just beginning to manage my finances so that I could progress, but of course things aren't always easy breezy as they sound. And I learned that lesson first hard.

After the summer came to an end, I had gotten dismissed from my duties at Old Navy, but I was still working at Virgin Megastore. Due to my limited income, things got a little shaky when it came to paying my bills. I got paid every two weeks, and I got paid just enough to pay my car note and insurance with one check, and enough for rent with the next check. Fortunately where I was staying, I was being provided food already so that wasn't something I had to worry about.

During this time there was one instance where I had agreed to assist a little more by paying a little extra one month for rent because the mortgage was due and the friend I was staying with was depending on my contribution. I had a very difficult decision to make. This was my check that was meant for my car note and insurance, and my mom had made very clear to me if I was over three days late she would repossess my car from me because she cosigned for it and it would affect her credit. So I had to decide: do I pay the extra rent, and miss a car note risking having no transportation to get to the job that I was holding to make it possible to have a place to sleep and way to survive? Or do I pay for my car note, and compromise my relationship with my friend and my place to stay? Either way, a decision had to be made immediately.

I decided to pay my car note and insurance. My logic was the fact that I didn't want to lose my car, and I also didn't want to hear my mom's mouth about messing up her name or credit. I felt bad because after making this decision, I didn't know how to face the friend I was living with. He inquired about the payment and I lied saying I had it trying to buy time because I didn't know how to say I didn't have it. I eventually found that I disappointed him, and I put him in a very hard position because when it came down to it, I wasn't providing the money I was promising and it could've compromised our living.

Of course because I didn't have anything of my own, I wasn't able to clearly see the bigger picture. My friend was so disappointed and hurt by my lying to him about having the money, but we hadn't seen each other much because our work schedules conflicted with one another. I remember being on my way home from a very long work day, exhausted and I got a phone call from my friend asking me to come out. I didn't feel up to it, but he indicated that he would be stranded if I didn't because he didn't drive, so I told him I would stop by for a moment though I was extremely tired. The hang out spot that was popular was a bar called the Lodge in North Hollywood, and we would usually go on Thursday nights. This Thursday was a little different. You could even feel the difference in the air.

Once I got there this time, things felt weird. It felt to me as if I was being treated differently by my peers, my friend, and no one was really speaking to me. I was being avoided and ignored and I didn't really feel comfortable. After a while, I went up to my friend and I told him I was exhausted and wanted to go home and go to sleep. I am not sure if it was the alcohol or if it was just his anger, but for the first time, I saw hatred in his eyes and it was directed toward me. It seems like slow motion, that he took a long sip of his cocktail before facing me and saying (maybe a little out of context),

"So what happened to the money you promised me? You know you could've compromised much more than just yourself by not keeping your word. This could compromise our living stability because you lied! That is fucked up, especially after all that I've done for you. What happened to the money? Why lie?"

I replied that I needed to pay my car note. He asked

"Is your car more important than a place to sleep? A place to stay? Food? Your priorities are fucked up! Are you happy? Do you feel you made the right decision?" Then he began really going in deeper and cutting with his words, speaking of how I had nothing at all, and how much he had helped me, and how I didn't appreciate it. He pointed out that everything I had on was stuff that he had bought for me, and that I had the nerve to disrespect him the way I did after all that he had done for me. The whole time he was chewing me out I literally felt like the entire club/bar was looking at me and laughing. It made me look like a fool.

I held my composure, though I felt broken and destroyed inside, I didn't show it, I just took it, and listened to him the entire time. He finished his confrontation by telling me that I needed to be out of the house by time he got there, and he planned on going directly there after the club. He also made sure to mention all the things he had given me or bought me and to be sure to leave those things too. Then he dismissed me and I walked out and to my car. I felt so broken, sad, hurt, damaged, embarrassed, and humiliated all at the same time.

I walked to my car trying my best to hold back my tears and to force a smile as familiar faces that were outside who greeted me with hellos and smiles. I felt like I was in a movie. What just happened? How did I make him this mad? I had never seen him like this. I felt so bad. Then it hit me, I have absolutely no where to go once I get my stuff out of his place. I hopped in my car and speed home - well what was my home - and I was determined to get all of my stuff out because I knew he was serious when he said I better be gone before he got there from the bar. I packed up my entire car with everything I owned within 25 minutes. I held it together. I had yet to even cry a tear over the situation because I was still in disbelief. I obviously made the wrong choice! As I grabbed the last of my items, I saw him walk into the house and he seemed to still be angry. So I wrote a note saying thanks for everything and I was taking the keys off of my key ring to leave them on the counter when he walked into the kitchen.

I was honestly terrified at this point because I didn't know what he was about to do. I thought he was going to fight me or something, but he just kinda stood there and stared at me. After I dropped the key on the counter, I said to him,
"Thank you for everything and I am sorry. He then gave me a hug saying that just because he wanted me out of his house didn't mean he wanted me out of his life. He said, "I don't hate you. I love you. One day you will understand. One day you will get it."

As he hugged me, I began to let out my first river of tears but I knew that I needed to go and figure out what I was going to do next. As I got in my car saying goodbye, I wiped my tears away and all I could do was try to play some music that would sooth the pain. It seemed like there was no song, no words, and no melody that could make me feel better about once again disappointing the very person who cared about me the most. I officially learned my lesson about the importance of keeping my word. I began wondering who I could call at 1:30 AM. Who would answer? I called one of my cousins, and she answered and said that I could stay the night, but that was all because she had other roommates that would have an issue with me staying there more than a night. I remembered asking my cousin for a blanket because I wanted to be able to cover up everything I had in my back seat so that people wouldn't be able to tell that I was now a residence of El Mirage (my car), at least until I found a new place to stay.

I woke up the next day and headed off to work. I couldn't even concentrate because there was so much on my mind. After work I went to my aunt's house. She lived in Pacoima and I wanted to speak with her. She looked surprised to see me but I was hoping she would allow me to stay with her until I figured out a plan. Unfortunately her response was,
"I don't even let my own son stay here for free, so I would have to ask of you the same thing I asked of him." I knew I didn't have the money and couldn't afford it, so I said 'thank you' and kept going.

Business at work was slowing down a little, and

so did my hours. I remember there was a time I went by another aunt's house who lived kinda near the North Hollywood area, and I had a cousin who was living with her, but I was hoping I would be allowed to occupy the other room she had that was a guest room. Well, that must not have sounded like a good idea, plus it may not have been fair of me to ask this of her, so I found myself spending another day sleeping in my car. I didn't tell any of my aunts the exact details of what I was dealing with. I was hoping they would take me in because we were related, but in life, things aren't always that easy. My other best friend lived in Sacramento at the time and he spoke to his mother about my situation and she offered me a chance to live with them. The only dilemma was that she lived an hour away from where I worked, and I only had enough gas to last me a month, and if I drove any further I wouldn't be able to afford to get back to work and of course work allowed me to pay my car note, which allowed me a place to sleep while I searched for a more permanent arrangement.

I was barely making ends meet. I started making just enough per month to pay my car note, insurance, fill up my gas tank and buy a family size bag of tortilla chips and a two liter Brisk Iced Tea. After that I was broke. This is what I survived on. I ended up living in my car for more than three months. I must say Monica's music and lyrics were my only peace of mind and way of making it through. That and my hope for a better day. I don't know what kept my faith so high through these times, but I surely didn't let it break me. I would park my car in places that I knew were safe and I knew I wouldn't be bothered. Sad to say the place I frequented was a spot down the street from one of my aunt's houses near North Hollywood because she lived in a good neighborhood, and I didn't think anyone would break into my car there. I would get up in enough time to find a local gas station that I could carry my hygiene bag into and freshen up for the day so that no one would ever know what I was enduring.

I was trying to explore my options, but it seems no one was trying to help right now or there was no room for me. I even contacted my biological dad once again, but there were too many people living in his house at the time. It's so interesting how strong I became throughout this time. I didn't cry much because all of my emotions were expressed through my writing and my music. I didn't understand at the time where my strength and courage came from. I didn't understand why I still had a great attitude at work and how I kept a smile on my face during this time. I guess I learned to wear a mask that would cover up all of the things I really was going to expose to everyone else.

The mask I wore covered up a multitude of things; pain, disappointment, hurt, low self-esteem, mistakes, disease, abandonment, loss, rejection, struggle, fear, sadness, relationships, being misunderstood, pride, family, suicide, perception, judgment, forgiveness, depression, acceptance, sexuality, insecurities, homelessness, lack of trust, disrespect, addiction, and confrontation. It's so interesting that when a person sees you they assume you are happy or everything is great because they see you smile, but they have no idea what you really may be going through. I guess I did a great job! I say that because my mask really had people convinced, and they really started to believe that what they saw was what it really was. No one really knew what was behind the mask.

If only someone would have looked a little deeper. Deeper into my eyes and much deeper behind my smile, they would've seen the pain and the real me. No one cared to take that time, so when they looked at me and saw me smile, with this well-developed illusion of a smile, all they saw on the outside a perception of who they thought I was. I imagined they thought I exuded strength, faith, happiness, success, joy, support, independence, confidence, love, power, peace, fulfillment, empowerment, courage, achievement, determination, hope, awareness, drive, self-esteem, security, family, truth, connection, balance, beauty, health, admiration, money, understanding, knowledge, inspiration and clarity. This could not have been further from the truth.

Finally a day came where my smiling mask cracked. It was September 11th, 2001. It was crazy! This was something that impacted the entire world and that included me. Business almost came to a complete halt after that day and half of us at Virgin Megastore were laid off. I had no clue what I would do now. How was I gonna pay my car note? At this point, it's not just a car note, but everything I owned was in my car and this was where I laid my head to sleep. What was I gonna do? First thing I thought about was my mom because if I am late on this car note, I know she had to do what she had to do and I would have nowhere to go. I had no money saved and I couldn't think of any options.

My best friend in Sacramento came up with another solution. He told me about a couple of girls who lived in the dorms at California State University of Northridge (CSUN) and after he spoke to them, they let me stay there for a couple of nights. These girls were so cool we hit it off right away. The agreement we made was that I would apply to get food stamps and that I would buy food for the household and help them with their homework if they allowed me to sleep on their couch. It worked out and things were cool. Well, until the month came to an end and I had to admit to my mom that I didn't have the money to pay for the car. She made some arrangements. Not to help me pay the note because that clearly was not a part of our agreement but to come pick up the car. She had someone in mind who she could sell the car to who would take over the payments so they wouldn't fall behind. I had to take everything I owned and put it in the coat closet that everyone had access to in the dorm room. Another chapter, another journey.

The interesting thing was I took these hurdles and obstacles in stride. I didn't seem to panic too much because I felt as if I was becoming numb to all of the hardships. I felt like I was at the bottom, so I didn't expect much and I didn't find much that surprised me. Honestly, I didn't realize the amount of faith I had and that I was showing this in the ways I dealt with my situations. I just kept going because I knew that being at the bottom, the only place left to go was up.

This was also a chapter in my life that I truly learned from. It got quite interesting, active and uncomfortable after while at the dorm. I was there for a few months, and things started getting uneasy. I felt as if I was no longer wanted there. I always felt as if I was being treated differently and I just needed to figure something out. They would always have guests over and since I slept on the couch, I always had to wait until everyone left before I could even go to sleep. To get away when they had their company, I would just take long walks and try to kill time. There was only so much walking I could do and it became kinda frustrating, especially the times I was exhausted from the job hunting and interviews I was going on.

One particular night I remember feeling really frustrated with my living situation and I was trying to figure out what my next steps should be. I walked down this street I hadn't explored before and all of a sudden, I heard singing, and it sounded amazing. I was very intrigued and had to see where this was coming from.

Living Praise Christian Center was the name of the amazing place I found. It was a church that was located right down the street from where I was staying. I began spending every moment I could at this church. After a while, I ended up getting saved here. My first time receiving the Holy Spirit and speaking in tongues was here. I was baptized here as well. I always knew there was a God and I believed in him, but never to this degree I felt after I was saved. I would talk to God, but I didn't know much about what a relationship with God was supposed to be. I learned quickly though. This was the best thing that had ever happened to me.

There was one key message that stood out to me the most and it pretty much indicated that "If you don't like the situation you're in, God has already given you all the tools you need to get out of it." I took this to mean where I was staying. I remember calling my mom the next day. She was at work, but I was letting her know that I had nowhere to go and I wanted to know if she would allow me to come back to her home. She told me she had to ask my dad and that she would let me know. I reiterated that I had nowhere else to go, and she told me to come on and we would figure it out. Mind you, this was also the day that my dorm roommates decided they didn't want me or any additional bodies in their dorm anymore. I called a cousin who was always very loving and helpful to me and she allowed me to use her car for the day. All I had to do was take her to work and be back in time to pick her up. So I did. I dropped her off in Pasadena, went to the dorms, packed up all of my stuff in her car, and drove it out to Lancaster. I met with my mom. Though I could tell my parents didn't really want me back in their house they allowed me to move back. I dropped off my stuff and drove back down to get my cousin from work.

Unfortunately I felt very uncomfortable at my parent's house this time around. I think it was their strategy to make me hurry up and get my stuff together so I could get out. I wasn't allowed to eat any of their food, not even a piece of bread that I didn't buy. I would have to sneak food in order to eat. I was expected to leave the house every day at 9am, and I couldn't come back until after 6pm. This taught me discipline but also assured that I had time to kill. I assume my parents figured it would encourage me to look for jobs.

The city of Lancaster is quite spread out and I didn't have a dime to my name so I couldn't get a bus to get anywhere. The places I was able to apply were limited. I was really going through it and at times it felt like it was no better than me sleeping in my car. After a while, I found myself starting to steal my step dads change out of his change jar so that I could eat or get bus fare so that I could go beyond what was within walking distance. Of course he knew but I also lied about it. How do I say I needed his money so that I could eat because I have no other way?

My mom was nice enough to allow me to eat some of her stuff sometimes. It would always be after my dad went to work. He worked the graveyard shift. I grew up thinking he hated me. We had such a complex relationship. I learned a lot from this experience. It taught me about responsibility and striving for independence. Though I didn't understand it at the time, I can now say I appreciate the life lessons that I was learning during that time.

It seemed at the time that all the relationships in my life failed. I felt like I destroyed everything I touched. Family ties, friendships, romantic relationships. If this is what life is going to be like, I was waiting for the gift to be revealed because I was truly struggling and I was praying that this struggle would somehow pay off in the end. I remember when I began recognizing how much faith I had, and it actually happened in the most interesting way. Throughout all the obstacles I was facing I kept my faith even when I didn't know what Faith with a capital

F was. God supplied me with it!

Poetry
When I was on the wrong path
You brought me to the right road
Your love- to me
Is worth more than gold…
…And I hold
You close and near
No matter what I go through I know you are here.

Spirituality and Faith are more descriptive of the connection I feel to a higher power. It's hard for me to conceptualize religion beyond spirituality. I'm talking about my spirit. It's like speaking of my heart. It is the foundation behind something precious to me. It's a way of life.

Faith is a whole other thing. It's not too hard having faith in God because I know I'm here for a greater purpose. Where my faith tends to waiver is in finding and attaining real love and an everlasting relationship with someone who fully supports, loves and understands me. Including all my flaws — my status, insecurities and mood swings. I know I have issues, but I need a person who won't judge me for them and who can help me through them. I tend to lack faith in myself at times.

My faith waivers but a lot of it has to do with my confidence and self-esteem because those elements are not always there. Faith in love is a question. I know my ability to love, but the love I am able to receive is another thing.

In the past the inability of others to love me effectively made me question the love I was deserving of. Could I be faithful but not full of Faith? So I went to church, and after hearing the message, these are the notes I took:

* Who you associate with makes a big difference as to where you're going and how fast you get there.

*Honor God no matter what position or situation you're in. He Can Fix All Things. He Reigns, He Loves, He Delivers, He Heals, He Saves, He Helps, He Strengthens, And He Forgives. He is Good! He is God! Give it to God. He's the only one that can turn things around and change your situation. Again, He Reigns! No weapons formed against us will prevail. No Negativity, No Disease, Nothing! Declare what you went through yesterday to be over today. God is too mighty for you not to get through.

*We need to operate in the principle of acknowledgement. God may not like some things we do or some things about us; but he loves us unconditionally. Therefore He allows us to lose some things (to get us where we should be). He's going to purge us; Do some cutting and clipping. God may get rid of some people or relationships this year so we can get on with God's business. Let Him do his thing! Just obey. God is using us. If we keep the unworthy in our lives, that's the devils way of holding us back. The devil is the one that will keep us out of church, allowing us to think we're being God to ourselves, and we haven't a fractional amount of abilities that God has.

*When we feel we are standing alone, God is carrying us. We can't doubt that, or deny Him of that. Stay hooked and connected to God for without Him, we can't do anything. We have to acknowledge the foolishness we have allowed into our lives. Don't blame God for it. Give God his credit, and He will bless. Acknowledge all that He does in our lives. We have to allow God to shine through us. God gives us boldness and power, but if we're weak in faith, we easily fall. God shows up when we acknowledge Him and call on Him. We have to name it to claim it!

*If we leave an inch, the devil takes a mile. We gotta stay strong with the Lord. We gotta stay strong with the Lord. We have to also acknowledge all the little things God does to get things in store for us. Take chances when it comes to what's deserved of us. God will back us up if we stay righteous, prayed up, and acknowledge God's doing. Recognize what He's doing for us now, if it's not all we may want, we're not appreciating what all is being done. Take one step at a time.

*The ways God is reaching us in our lives are: Faith, Prophecy, and Principle (obedience to God's word). No one but me can dictate to my outcome. Stay with God, I should have no worries. Obey God's Principles completely! Then we shall find success. Allow love & loyalty to show like a necklace. Write them in our minds and hearts. Then spiritually your success has already begun. If you float with the Principles; the blessings will come to pass.

*Have a balance of mercy and truth. Don't judge. Don't be taken advantage of. You can't save and rescue everyone, because then they'll become so dependent upon you. You need to find that balance. Hold some people to a standard. Let them hit their head a few times or they won't do anything on their own. You'll find yourself living life just to help them.

*Say "no" sometimes. It may help in the end. Don't try to save the world; you'll allow those not helping themselves to bring you down too. Get your life straight. You're not where you should be, but if you don't get your life together you'll stay there. Unless God purges that tree it will not bear anymore fruit!

CHAPTER 8
Finding a New Direction

Some days of my life are much more fulfilling than others, but I learned you can't always drive the car. Sometimes you have to ride, so you learn to embrace each turn and bump along the long ride toward your destination. You also may find that relaxing and trusting in the driver makes the ride a much more comforting one. And after driving for so long I decided it was time that I give God back the keys and let him drive 'cause truthfully only He knows where I'm going.

Life is funny. I mean sometimes I feel at my best and at other times I could be at my lowest point, but no matter how I am feeling or what I'm going through life still goes on with or without me. Sometimes I'll smile, sometimes I'll cry, but the reality of life will always be whatever it is. There was one day that was really "different" for me. I took a lot of time to just think and analyze "Me.

I was going through a whirlwind of emotions and it was pretty weird. I was broke, homeless, car-less, yet I felt free. I knew I got sad and depressed sometimes but I just felt free! I got lonely but I had people who loved me and I was free. So why did I complain? Why did I fight myself? Why did I whine? I was free. I may not have had all that I wanted or all that I longed to have but the reality was I was blessed. I was sane, in my right mind, intelligent, smart, handsome, and I was free!

Everyone goes through hard times similar to what I was going through but you know what? I ate every day and I still had blessings and privileges others couldn't even begin to imagine so it definitely could have been worse. I know the Lord, my Father, never left me for dead. I may have gone through far more than I'd wanted to go through but He blessed me with the strength to endure and remain secure despite everything. I thanked God every day for all he had instilled in me. I found that survivor mentality and I kept fighting and wouldn't give up, especially when I knew there was a prize waiting for me at the end. There was one book that I read during that time in my life that especially helped me (it still does) about gaining strength during the challenges of life while building a spiritual relationship with God. That book was *Spiritual Warfare: Equipping the Christian Believer for Spiritual Warfare by Tobaise Brookins*.[6] The book changed my life.

Going through life's situations sometimes seemed to be much more difficult when it was something I dealt with or encountered alone. When I could have someone to stand by my side or fight along with me, it may felt a bit easier to endure my struggles. I truly feared being alone.

How could I know when and how to develop a healthy, lasting gay relationship if I had never seen positive examples of one? Is this the reason I had become so needy? So clingy? I mean to long for or feel the need of love in my life led me to encounter so

---

[6] *Spiritual Warfare: Equipping the Christian Believer for Spiritual Warfare* by Tobaise Brookins. 296 pages. Published by Gates Alliance 2009.

many different unhealthy situations but they were an expression of how empty I was feeling inside.

The longing I had to be loved sometimes led to being mistreated to have companionship, temporary fulfillment, and validation. Another bad thing I went through was being so afraid of being alone that I allowed myself to be cheated on or disrespected, all because I didn't want to be alone any more.

How could I establish or develop a strong, healthy relationship with myself when I let so many others diminish me and treat me so bad that I became blinded about my own true worth and value? How could I know what I deserve when I had never accessed it?

My relationship with myself was a big determining factor of what I expected or what my standard was when I was developing relationships with others. I found that what needs to happen first is that I needed to:

-Develop a strong relationship with God.
-Learn to identify how to place people in my life and define their role and my relationship with them.
-Build my relationships based on truth and reality.
-Stop abusing myself.
-Recognize when a relationship was not healthy.

I know this sounds easy but for me it wasn't simple. The biggest challenge about these key things for me was fear. I learned that fear stood for False Evidence Appearing Real. I came to realize one of the things I had feared most in my life was being alone. What was strange was that without even realizing it I found myself going to drastic measures to feel wanted when what I really wanted was simply to connect with someone or something. The reason the fear felt so devastating was because for many years I did not realize that God was at my side. It took the times He arranged for me to be by myself to learn much more about myself and to begin to understand how to cope with my fear. How could I be alone when God was with me?

In all of my failed attempts at love, God's love was always with me. So it made me question, did I really fail? I know that with each miserable experience I gained knowledge and wisdom and learned more about myself. I figured out what it was I sought from others in the relationships I was pursuing. I learned that I may feel lonely when others didn't get or understand me, but some things aren't for them. The loneliness was simply made for me to gain some understanding or insight. Through all of the revelation, I must admit, I still didn't like to be alone and this led to many mistakes in my life.

Let me tell you about another time I fell in love. I feared trusting and opening up to people because I still felt very insecure and I didn't think anyone would ever make me feel comfortable enough to, but I met this special someone and they proved me wrong. I met this guy at a club that I used to go to called The Arena Night Club in Hollywood. I thought he was really cute but I still feared being rejected and hurt so

I just smiled at him. I played it cool. This was a night I really wasn't having a great time. The music wasn't that great, and the people I came with were having a good time, so I just had to take one for the team and deal with it. I kept smiling and occasionally making eye contact with the cute guy then after while he approached me and began flirting with me.

He asked for my number and I felt like Jada Pinkett in *Set it Off* when Blair Underwood was trying to sweep her off of her feet. I started to think maybe there was hope for me. It was not that often that someone approached and or asked for my number, so this was new to me. I was intrigued so I gave him my number.

This boy and I would be on the phone for hours and hours day after day. He either had really good game or I was really naive because he knew the right things to say to make me feel like he was everything I hoped and dreamed of. At the time I lived between Lancaster and my friend's house in the San Fernando Valley. After a couple of weeks of talking, he began inviting me over to stay the night at his house, where he lived with his uncle. It didn't take me more than two months to be head over heels for this guy. I mean, he made me feel as if I was the only one that existed when I was with him.

The first time I spent the night with him, he told me that he wanted me to be his boyfriend, and that he thought he was falling in love with me. Of course I agreed to be his boyfriend. I couldn't understand what it was but I felt I could truly trust him. He was different from what I was used to though that wasn't saying much. It was as though he broke down every wall I had spent years building and he made me feel I was worthy of being loved.

That first night he cooked dinner for me, and he gave me a massage. I felt a little uncomfortable near bed time because he slept naked and we had to sleep in the same bed and I was kind of timid and afraid to have sex with him. I wasn't all that experienced, and I didn't know what he expected. As he started to give me a massage I began getting more comfortable and before I knew it he had me out of my clothes in bed with his arms around me.

One thing about the young "me" liking boys was that it was very rare back then that a parent would talk their child about sexuality or educate them about sex. Especially gay sex! I didn't know much about it, and I wasn't introduced to gay internet, porn or sex tapes until a later stage in my life. Most of my sex "know how" came from having sex so I didn't have much. My sexual relationship with this new boyfriend was a no-limitation type of raw sex. Raw sex meaning unprotected. No limitations, no short cuts. He seemed well versed with his sexual experience, and didn't mind guiding and showing me how to elevate my level of expertise.

He had a very large dick I thought was about 12 inches. He had a cute body and a very sensual nature about him. He took my limited experience and molded me into who he wanted me to be sexually. Before I knew it, we were more frequent and it seemed to get a bit rougher. I'm not sure I really enjoyed having sex, but I knew it was what I was supposed to be doing, right? I mean, I am here in a relationship and I knew I was supposed to love pleasing my man, right? He taught me every role, position, and approach to the sexual experiences he was introducing me to. His pleasure became my pleasure and I would overlook or not over-think the fact that every time he would play the dominating role when we had sex, I would start to bleed. He literally would tear me up and tell me that it was normal.

I dated him for eight months. Let me repeat that I dated HIM for eight months. Just because I was dating him, didn't mean he was dating me. Another life lesson that was hard to accept. It's often that a person will fall in love with the idea or potential of a person as opposed to who they truly are. I believed that because I was loyal and faithful to him that he had the same concept of our relationship and that he had the respect for me that I did for him. That turned out to be not true. This was something that I found out one night when he was in town and wanted us to go out clubbing.

I say he was in town because shortly after we started dating he told me he had been discovered by a modeling agent and that the modeling contract he was offered meant he would have to move to Chicago for few months to work. For me this was bittersweet but I wanted to be supportive. Maybe I didn't know as much as I thought about the modeling world. I thought you had to be a certain height or have a sculpted body to be discovered, but maybe it was his lucky day. When he mentioned this to me, he said he would still be able to come back here for the holidays and stuff, but that he really wanted to do this and that he wanted my support. Of course I was going to support him! He was my man! So he left. It seemed that the distance only created a greater divide between us. It wasn't often I was able to talk to him or get him on the phone. I know there's a time difference, but it seemed our times and schedules always conflicted. I tried to be patient and I didn't complain though I didn't like the situation much.

Over the course of months, I saw him from time to time when he came back into town, and I would ask him to show me some of the pictures from the modeling he had been doing. I don't know why, but he always said the photographer never sent them and that he could not reach him. He always had an excuse, and never any photos. It started to feel a bit weird to me. I didn't understand it, but I knew it wouldn't be long before I could see them, so I just stopped asking and focused on the little bit of time I got with him.

So this particular night we went out to the club. Usually when we were around one another, we were always quite affectionate but when we got to the club that night he wouldn't hold my hand. Throughout the night he would disappear to go talk to friends but he wouldn't introduce me. This was a lot different from the man I remembered. So I didn't enjoy myself one bit. At the time I was driving so when I look back at it maybe he was using me for rides 'cause I was like his driver or something. I took him everywhere he wanted to go.

Finally I knew I was ready to go home and I was mad because I had to take him home first. After leaving the club he asked me to go to this donut shop on Santa Monica and Highland, because he wanted to get something to drink. When we got there he asked me to go in with him. We got out of the car we saw a mutual friend. Not only did I not know they knew each other I was surprised when they started kissing in front of me to greet one another.

My "boyfriend" went inside to get something to drink, so I asked our mutual acquaintance how they knew each other. The response shocked me because he said that they had been dating on and off for three years. He then said,
"He's my boyfriend." I felt so stupid that I just replied with an "oh." So "our" boyfriend comes back out of the donut shop and we head back to the car so I can take him home and then I went home myself. My mind was blown and it was like I was in a daze or something. We didn't have a chance to talk about how I was feeling because he left town the next day. I just kept it all inside. I was so hurt.
It got a little weird when he returned to Chicago. He again stopped calling me or returning my calls. It was like he disappeared. Ironically, when he disappeared, I started hearing increasingly stuff about him. Things he was doing, people he was doing, rumors, and more. I didn't know what to feel or what to believe. He said that he loved me, so this couldn't be true, could it? I didn't want to believe any of the rumors until one day a friend and I were in West Hollywood and he said he wanted to show me something at the sex store.

Though apprehensive, I followed him inside and he showed me a cover of one of the porno videos. As I looked at the box, I saw my boyfriend's face on the cover in a position I never knew he even tried. My friend then showed me two other boxes and told me that he had found out earlier that day and didn't know how to tell me. He then said that there was more and that he would show me the next day. I was in total disbelief and shock! I didn't know how to respond or react, so I tried my best not to. This was like a movie! Who does this happen to?

Well, he didn't lie, the next day my friend took me to a site called CoCo Dorms. This was a site where there were a multitude of guys that lived in this alleged dorm with each other, and they would have sex, jack off sessions and threesomes live on camera for people to pay and watch. They had it down to an agenda of what to expect at what times, and they would have scenes in different areas of this dorm. I never knew stuff like this existed, but what shocked me the most was when my friend logged in and I saw my boyfriend's profile.

Now I was in shock and I saw that he was scheduled to be live the next day. I couldn't believe this could be real, so I tried calling him and his phone went straight to voicemail. I was livid! I ended up not getting to talk to him until two days later. When we talked, we had a long conversation. I had to confront him because I was not about to be played. I loved him, but I needed an explanation. I went off! He was kinda surprised by my confronting him, but he must've known I was a fragile, naive, low self-esteem boy who was afraid to be alone because he conjured up some story and shut me right up. It was along the line of how old those tapes supposedly were and how there was a time he was homeless and had to do that to make money to survive.

So then I asked him about the live website. He then said that he didn't want to tell me because he thought he would lose me and that he was about to quit. He said that it was everyone else that had sex and threesomes, and that all he did was jack off on camera and that it was only to make money so we could get an apartment together when he came back to LA. He then gave me a one day password that would allow me to see his session so I could see there was nothing to worry about, and he also told me he would wink into the camera so that I knew it was for me.

He said that though he was doing this, it meant absolutely nothing and that no one but me would have him. I know this all sounds crazy, but I was dumb enough to eat up every word. I believed him. I asked him about our mutual friend, and he told me that boy was lying. He said the reason I don't hold your hand in clubs is because there's a lot of people that like me and they can't have me and they're gonna be mad at you because you have me and they can't. Why did I believe him? He also said that if I loved him I would stop listening to everyone else because they were just jealous.

I watched his session the next day and it was okay. I didn't like the idea of everyone being able to see him naked but he did give me the wink he promised. Though I was relieved it wasn't as bad as I first thought, there was still something I didn't trust. I stayed with him though.

A couple of weeks later he returned and things felt different. He still had me driving him everywhere but I was becoming fed up because he deliberately ignored me and did not even apologize about it. I was being neglected but I was still foolish enough to stick around. The last night I remember spending with him was one in which we got into heated arguments all night. We had rented a hotel room for the night so that we could spend some long overdue quality time that I had been asking for. Once we had gotten settled in the room he said a friend was gonna stop by.

Before I could even respond to his surprise announcement the friend was knocking on the door. I was irritated so I asked the friend to leave after five minutes of him being there. When the friend left my boyfriend got so mad he started strangling me. I fought back at first, but was so hurt I felt defeated and gave up. When he realized what he was doing to me, he got up and started crying, saying he was sorry and he only did that because he loved me so much and that only I had the ability to push his buttons 'cause I was the only one he ever let into his heart. I was still mad so I stayed over by the window in silent tears, then I glanced his way after moments of silence to notice that he started looking a little weird while lying on the bed. All I can remember was that he started to shake and I noticed his eyes were starting to roll in the top of his head.

I screamed, "Oh My God, are you ok? What's wrong? What's wrong?" He attempted to tell me he was having a seizure and I said "What am I supposed to do?" He pointed to a towel and I grabbed it, poured some cold water on it, and put it on his forehead. He then had me put pillow behind his head. He then kept shaking uncontrollably as he lay on the floor. It was one o'clock in the morning but I was so scared I called my mother.

"Mom, my friend is having a seizure and I don't know what to do! I'm so scared." She said, "Why are you calling me, you need to call 911, what do you want me to do?" She was right. I hung up with her and asked him how he was doing and said that I was about to call 911. He then started coughing saying that he was okay now the seizure had passed and that he had them all the time. He said that there was no need to call 911 he just needed to lie down. I forgot about what we were arguing about and began holding him not realizing it would be the very last time that I would.

No, he didn't die. The bastard was still alive. Though I finally forgave him for all he did to me I ended our relationship the next day because I couldn't get past the lies and surprises. He didn't seem to care much either. I should've known something was wrong when I had introduced him to one of my best friends and my best friend told me that there was something wrong with him and that I need to leave him ASAP. He just felt it, and told me that my boyfriend wasn't a good person. I was head over heels at the time and didn't listen. I stuck with him and it ended up going nowhere. At least I gave love a try. It still hurts to think about him to this day. Why does it hurt so bad?

After we separated, I started getting random calls from random boys. Some threatened to fight me while others tried to have sex with me because we connected after realizing that they had been hurt by him too. I was just over this relationship. Sometimes it hurts to do the very things that are necessary for your life. No matter how he hurt me, I still felt love for him, and I don't understand why. What is it when you've become so accustomed to pain that you're numb to it? I allowed the same pains to be inflicted on me because I was familiar with that feeling or I knew the level of pain I could endure. Does that make it okay, I asked myself? No! Love is not meant to hurt. I was not meant to be lied to and cheated on.

Though I've only shared a few of the things that happened to me, I swear I've been hurt so much in my life that it came to be something expected. Not that I deserved it but it seemed to be all that I knew, whether it was my feelings from how people mistreated me or hurt from being disappointed time and time again. It got to a point where I had cried so much I had no more tears. I didn't want to hurt anymore. How could I stop the hurt? Was there anything else besides hurt for me to feel? It hurts....

I hurt... I hurt ... how could I heal? I was alone once again. Loneliness was knocking on my door and I was walking toward the door to turn the damn knob.

It didn't help that the next day would be Valentine's Day! I could see people acting all lovey-dovey because of this ridiculous, exaggerated, overrated holiday. If I loved someone, weren't they supposed to show me love every day not just one day of the year? Why did someone create a day to tell you to buy flowers and stuff for the person you supposedly love? That makes no sense. Let me tell you what the Day means to me. Let me tell you about my funny

Valentine.

CHAPTER 9
My Funny Valentine

It's Valentine's Day again. You know what's crazy -- I never had a Valentine. I would always consider my mom to be my Valentine, because this day is supposed to be geared around and based on love. I never doubted (well, maybe sometimes) that my mom loved me. A big part of the lessons in my life came from my pursuit of love. I have always felt that everyone wants to be loved and that everyone deserves to be loved.

It seems that in each relationship I got into I became increasingly disappointed with love's progression. I guess it's something people learn to deal with over time. My greatest lesson was discovering that God is love and the love I felt I was missing was because I wasn't looking to Him as an option or a resource for me. I was learning. There were times I'd lose focus of the true essence of what love was. I would get the feeling that the person I was into was really into me too. I did my share of dating. Well, to clarify, I didn't do real dating, I called dating as myself trying to get to know someone until they got what they wanted out of me (sex). What I found was that things would drastically shift and change from the time we would meet to when I had the feeling he might be falling for me to the part where we started having sex.

I am definitely a romantic at heart, but despite the 100% I always gave to nurture the relationship, I never seemed to get even remotely close to that amount of effort in return. I made myself believe that if I gave my all, and I mean every bit of my being-, 100% of me - to someone I could then hope that they'd give at least half that much in return. I wanted someone to give me 100%. But without recognizing my own worth or what I deserved, I felt I had to overcompensate with my effort in order for me to be deserving of someone's "all.

I'd like to think I'm an attractive dude. I am 6'0 tall, medium brown complexion, regular build, not skinny, not heavy, not muscular, and not frail. I have a nice smile, mesmerizing eyes (at least that's what I've been told). My personality, I feel, hints at the levels of greatness within me. I am a good person and once I expose my heart people seem to be attracted to or interested in me. But in the end they just don't do right by me.

Well, it was Valentine's Day again, and all I could do was sit there and reminisce about my many failed relationship attempts and my many lessons learned. If I had to give advice to anyone, I would say never allow yourself to be validated only by the appreciation one person shows you. I had to learn to love myself first and consider another person showing love toward me just icing on my cake. I know that no one can love me in all the ways I love me. But I also wondered if I'd learned that lesson too late. So on this Valentine's Day it kind of made me sick that everywhere I looked I saw displays of flowers, teddy bears and the overrated media hype of what the day was supposed to look like. Who came up with these so-called "ideal expressions of love" for Valentine's Day anyway?

Okay, of course this was just my opinion and maybe it was coming from a bitter place because I had never had a "Valentine" or someone to show me the "expressions of love" that everyone else was bragging about. I spent most of my life single, so maybe it was just a longing I had for companionship. I wouldn't have minded someone thinking of me or sending me flowers. But the thing is I would rather have those sentiments given to me on a regular day over Valentine's Day. I wanted to know someone loved me because they did, not because it was the time of the year that they were obligated "express their love" to me. This overrated made-up holiday that was supposed to be dedicated to showing love and affection was the day that so many people acted as if their dysfunctional relationships were perfect. It seemed like people spent hundreds of dollars to do the very things they didn't intend on doing the rest of the year. It seemed to me that if they didn't buy into the hype then they thought their significant other would have a fit because they wanted to also experience the feeling of love that all of their friends and coworkers were gushing that they felt. It seemed that people truly believed that they could make up for their failed expressions on other 364 days of the year on that one day. What bullshit.

One thing I didn't understand was why is it that whenever this time of the year came and I knew it was just that false commercial hype, I always felt so lonely? Why was I always alone, always by myself? Honestly, loneliness hurts a lot. I felt lonely to the point where I didn't want to breathe, live, or be alive anymore because every single moment that I was alive seemed to provide another opportunity for pain to come in. Well, that's how I felt right then. And it seemed like it felt worse whenever it came to Valentine's Day even though I knew I shouldn't.

I was in my early twenties and I was in an interesting transition period in my life. Though I wasn't necessarily wanted there, I had to move back home for a short time with my parents again. It was that time of the year, right after the holidays, but the weather seemed colder than usual. I was depressed and I also had to deal with a dang cold that I couldn't seem to shake. I swear it felt like I had been coughing for an entire month. I was having problems sleeping, a loss of appetite, I was feeling weak, felt as if I could barely walk, cold sweats, and was constantly throwing up and in the restroom with diarrhea. I felt like I was dying! This was crazy. I remember there were times I would be in the shower or brushing my teeth and I would just black out and faint. I would wake up with a weird tingle in my body and then come around back to normal again. I assumed it was because I wasn't eating much, so I just ignored it. The symptoms seemed like a stomach virus to me. It was right after the holidays so I thought maybe I ate too many plates or something. I thought the leftovers must've caught up to me. This "stomach virus" lasted for about a month before I started getting worried.

One day I was running back and forth to the restroom because I felt like I had to go, but each time I would sit down all that would come out was blood. I knew this wasn't normal and after a week of this I decided to tell my mom. She asked me if I was constipated because I surely ate a whole lot of macaroni and cheese. We tried milk of magnesia and prune juice thinking it would help me go to the bathroom easier. Well, it didn't work. By this time my mom suggested I go to the hospital. I went to the hospital and they tried every test they could to figure out what the heck was wrong with me. They didn't know and couldn't understand what was up with my symptoms. They wanted to make sure it wasn't something more serious than just constipation or flu so the doctor ran more tests. We went home because we had to wait for the test results to come back from the lab.

On February 14th, 2005, ironically Valentine's Day, I received the phone call that told me that the results from my blood work. The doctor said that I needed to schedule an appointment to come in as soon as possible. Before he hung up the doctor revealed to me that I was HIV Positive and that it was important that I come in within the next day or two. The words bounced in my skull like a ricocheting bullet but in slow motion. Was he even supposed to tell me this kinda stuff over the phone?

I had no idea what it meant. What exactly was HIV? Why did it sound so serious? I needed more information to understand what it was that I was dealing with. It felt eerie, like I could hear nothing but silence and my heartbeat. Everything seemed to be in slow motion, and I didn't know why I felt so numb as though I had lost all feeling in my body. I was in a trance while my mind tried to figure out how to process this news when I was not even sure what HIV meant. I was terrified Wow, Happy Valentine's Day to me. This is the day I found out I had HIV so it would be the day that changed my life forever.

I had to call to set my appointment and they gave me the 18th as my appointment day. This meant that I have four days to sit and wonder before I could get more information about what was going to happen to me. I think the craziest feeling in the world must be to hear that you have a deadly disease about which people are often stigmatized and not even know what being diagnosed with that disease really means. Did it mean I was going to die soon? Was it contagious? Honestly I had no idea what it meant. A million questions passed through my nearly frozen mind. What will this disease do? How long would I have it? How would I get better? Who else in my life has it? Who should I tell?

I think what I worried most about was how I was going to tell my mom and my best friend. I didn't know what to do, how to feel, what to think. I kind of just kept it to myself. I couldn't sleep, I didn't want to talk to anyone, and I didn't have an appetite at all. I was truly depressed. That night while reading a book, I just broke down and started crying. I cried to the point where I let out a lot of the worry and as the cries got softer I allowed my tears to lull me to sleep. My next tears didn't come until the night of the 18th when the reality set in that I was HIV-positive and that I probably would be for the rest of my life.

My mom took me to that doctor's appointment on the 18th, so I told my mom immediately after leaving the doctor about my status. I couldn't lie to her about it. After talking with her, I told her I didn't think I wanted to tell anyone. We decided that if people started seeing drastic changes in my appearance or anything, that we would just say that it was a form of cancer or something because that would be more acceptable than HIV. So that was my new diagnosis – cancer - but only if anyone noticed changes in my appearance or asked me about it. What's sad is trying to negotiate which deadly disease I would rather claim to have in order to gain acceptance from others because of negative perceptions of HIV-AIDS.

My mom was totally supportive and encouraged me throughout the whole ordeal. I knew that she was really in a lot of pain and hurting for me, but she only showed it through love and strength. My mom was the type of person who would never let you see her cry. She had one of the biggest hearts and she was also more sensitive than she would let people know. But I could say she never let me see her cry even though I had disappointed her terribly and she was hurting from it. I would get sad every time I looked at her 'cause I felt as if I deprived her of so much. I am gay so from me she would probably not get a grandchild, and then I was HIV-positive so she might have to bury one of her kids before herself. I really had failed her.

Also at that fateful appointment on February 18th, I found out that on top of HIV I also had syphilis. The doctor told me that it would've soon traveled to my brain and caused me to go insane if I hadn't found out when I did. I was given penicillin shots which treated the syphilis. Treatment for the HIV was a whole other thing and something I would have to live with for the rest of my life.

At that time in the Palmdale area there were no HIV specialists. Trying to get treatment for the disease was hell. I was trying so hard without knowing how to navigate through the health and medical services world that it became extremely discouraging. All the information was out there for people, but if someone like me had no idea about how to access it or what exactly I should be looking for I could not find it. Was I the only one who had no idea or information about HIV? This was true even when I went to the same doctor again to ask him questions. All he did was hand me a pamphlet and told me to call the number that was on it saying they *might* be able to help me.

I called the number immediate when I left his office only to be disconnected. If that number didn't work I didn't know where to turn. My mom encouraged me to check the Internet to find out more about where to go for support and further treatment. How did people live with this disease when everyone, even the doctors, didn't want to deal with it? Facing the look of disgust that people got when they heard those three letters together was shocking and so discouraging. It shouldn't have been a surprise. Folks living with the virus would rather keep it to themselves because they didn't want to be looked at like plague victim. Who would want to be treated like an alien or a science experiment? It made no sense. In just one week after my diagnosis I had already seen how many people didn't want to deal with or help me even if they were getting paid to do so! With my Internet research I found that most of the information and assistance was based in the Los Angeles areas o I

knew this was where I would have to go if I wanted to
get help.

A couple of days after getting a prescription from
the doctor I finally decided to get it filled. When I went
to pick up the prescribed medications found out one
them cost $248.00 dollars. The other cost $738.00. I
can't even tell you how quick I walked up outta that
pharmacy! You would have thought I was the speed-
walking champion of the USA and that I was
undefeated and was in the midst of a competition.
That was crazy! So the doctor told me I was pretty
much going to die because there was no one willing
to help me, and if I wanted to stay alive I would have
to pay all this money that I did not have. Not just once
but every 30 days for pills that also had a long list of
side-effects that read like a horror novel from Barnes
and Noble. And that was just the beginning! Was this
what my life was going to be like? And from what I
understood, my treatment would get even much more
expensive than that. I didn't know what I was going to
do.

I began going through so many different
emotional stages and I can't pretend that the
adjustment was easy for me. It was a struggle. It was
hard to want to live another day only to realize my
disease was just getting worse. I lost a lot of my
strength, courage, motivation, and drive but I had to
try to get it back. I had to remind myself of reasons I
should want to be alive.

I went through denial thinking my diagnosis could
not be true! I must have been dreaming. This couldn't
be my life. Why me? Maybe I should get a second
opinion or something because this wasn't fair. What

did I ever do to deserve this? I wanted to believe I would wake up and this would have just been a nightmare. Well it wasn't and once I realized this really was my reality, I went through a stage where I experienced extreme sadness and isolation. I started thinking as if I were living my last days on earth and that I would drop dead and die any day. This wasn't a healthy mindset, but I couldn't help but feel sad about how disappointed I was in myself and how many people I had let down.

I found myself telling people I loved them and preparing for the worse. I talked to my mom and told her how I wanted my funeral to look and what I wanted to be wearing. It was quite awkward. She didn't know how to engage in this conversation, but she listened 'cause she knew it was something I really wanted to share with her. I felt sorry for myself. I wrote every single day because I thought it would be best to journal my last days. This was followed by isolation. I tried to avoid everyone and everything because I didn't want to have to face the world. I didn't feel ready. In my mind I thought people would know I had HIV when they looked at me. As if it would be written all over my face or something. This was not fair.

I experienced a level of anger and blame that I would not have associated with who I was. I was mad at the person who did this to me. I hated him for this. Hated him for making me love him. I had to be mad at myself too because it does take two. I wanted to play grown up, so I should have known what I was getting into 'cause my life was my responsibility. I went through the bargaining stage where I was talking about the "shoulda, woulda and coulda" and the what-ifs. It didn't help at all because of course I couldn't turn back time and redo the things I wished I could have or should have.

I feared death and I went through some major anxiety and depression. Then I started to realize I just needed to stop trying to figure this all out at once. I had to simply pause. The crazy thing was throughout this time most of my depression still came from the thought that I would be deprived of love. I was depressed because I thought no one would ever want to be with me or date me because I was HIV-positive. What was I gonna do now? It was hard enough to get a man without this, now what kinda miracle would I have to pray for 'cause I would need some hope on my side.

I started driving myself crazy but at the same time thankfully I started finding resources and services that could help me deal. I learned to accept the things I could not change and to strive to find ways to cope with my diagnosis. I couldn't pretend that it was something easy to do, but I had to try to find the light within all of this darkness.

I wondered if I would ever achieve the goals I'd set for myself or if I would live long enough to love and be loved in return. Could I ever be happy? I didn't even know if I would tell anyone about my status. I thought I should tell people to let them know this could happen to anyone, but I didn't want to be treated differently. Who knew where my life would lead. Who even knew how much more life I had to live?

After getting my diagnosis, a big part of me died. I was no longer the person I was before I found out. The weird thing was that I was not even mad at my ex-boyfriend. It was my mistake for allowing him to have unprotected sex with me. I did not even know for sure that he was the one who gave it to me though I felt 99.9% sure.

It hurt that I had allowed my life to slip into somebody else's hands right through my own fingers. How could I now live a fulfilling life? I didn't even think it would be fair to date because my circumstance would put anyone I dated in a compromised position. Who would date someone who is HIV-positive? If a potential "date" looked at my life and saw what I saw or felt what I felt they would know I wasn't someone or something to brag about. I couldn't even remember the last time I had "really" smiled or "really" laughed. Anyone could just look into my eyes and see the pain, the hurt, my struggle and my heartache.

Why did it take something drastic to happen for me to fully value or appreciate my life? Now when I see people carelessly having unprotected sex I wonder if they will find it worth the gamble? Would I be HIV-positive if I had known how to prevent it? I wish I had the choice before getting infected. I guess I did have a choice, but more of a consciousness like after I was more educated. I swear when I first found out about my HIV-positive status I had no Idea what HIV was and I certainly had no clue what it would mean for my life or the adjustments I would need to make. The first thing I heard was that I was going to get AIDS and die. I assumed that meant I had a very short time left to live so I began living each day as if it were my last. And it made me wonder why I hadn't done so sooner.

In one of my favorite movies called *Last Holiday*

with Queen Latifah the main character has only a few weeks to live so every choice she makes is very important. It wasn't until I began living each day as if it were my last that I started appreciating every moment of life and valuing each person who crossed my path. I tried not to take much for granted and to savor every moment 'cause tomorrow was not promised. Why did I wait until I felt hopeless or thought I was gonna die soon to begin living?

Despite what I was going through emotionally I knew I had to leave my mother's house. It was time for me to figure out my next steps, so I went to Los Angeles to get health care services and support from the Minority AIDS Project (MAP). I was able to access their resources, information and support systems and that allowed me to understand how to deal with the disease I was now dealing with. I got linked to their health care services and I transitioned into a shelter so I wasn't homeless. While I waited for things to line up, one of my best friends allowed me to stay with him. While I stayed with him he held me accountable, making sure I followed up with the resources and programs I was trying to access.

I was so eager I would go to the MAP office every single day. I didn't want to wait for a call back, so I stayed up in their faces until they made some stuff happen, and they truly did! I was fortunate to finally feel as if my life was going to turn around and start becoming manageable. I actually looked forward to seeing what my future had in store for me. I was meeting new people. Some of those I met had lived a very long time with the disease. Some were just advocates for those living with HIV. It was an entirely new world, a world in which I didn't feel judged. Maybe life wasn't gonna be so terrible after all...

CHAPTER 10
Just Look into My Eyes

I can thank God that I am now alive, and there are no signs of my life ending anytime soon. People always ask me why I am so nice to people or why I am so giving, but my response is that life is too short not to be. Why should I be selfish, I can't take material things with me when it's time to go, so why hold value in material things as opposed to valuing the blessing that is having others in my life? I try to treat everyone well. I try to maintain positivity because negativity is draining and I can't afford to waste a moment of my life on things that are petty or that don't really matter to me.

There are so many people who are still becoming infected with HIV in our community. People think it's limited to being a 'gay disease,' or that if you are heterosexual you have nothing to worry about. That is false! A lot of the problem is lack of education as was my case. It's crazy that there is so much information that is accessible today but if you don't know what's there or you don't have a reason to research it how would you know?

Another problem is the sense of hopelessness that tends to exist in the black community, a community where so many find their friends and family are infected. Many people begin to believe that it's just a matter of time before it happens to them. Other people assume that they are invincible or believe that they aren't engaging in risky behaviors, so they never even get tested and don't know what their status is in the first place. This, of course, can lead to a person infecting many others without even realizing it.

HIV is killing us and people are afraid -- so afraid they'd rather act as if it doesn't exist, but denying it doesn't make it go away. Because they fear judgment or being rejected by loved ones, many people aware of their status still do not take part in health care services nor do they seek emotional support for coping. This is leading to higher rates of depression, suicide, and drug dependency in our community. This needs to change. We need to have deeper discussions and more open dialogue. We need to make our conversations about what it means to be HIV-positive a normal part of health discussions as well as discussing how to maintain our HIV-negative status along with the healthiest lifestyle possible.

When folks talk to their kids, nephews, nieces, sisters and brothers about sex, what is it exactly are they educating them about? Many times it's limited to "use a condom, or 'don't come home pregnant," but what about explaining in more detail why? What about STDs? What about HIV? What about really making sure loved ones fully understand what is happening out there when people are having unprotected sex. It's a cruel world especially for young people who find out they're HIV-positive.

I think the hardest thing for people who are HIV-positive to encounter is the stigma and the scrutiny of peers. People don't want to talk about it, and many more people go through life feeling no one understands or as if they are the only one going through this. What saddens me most is that many times, it is other people that are HIV-positive who make it a difficult transition for newly diagnosed HIV-positive individuals. I guess it is true that hurt people hurt people. HIV is not a death sentence, but it is imperative to tell anyone who isn't taking care of themselves, whether they are HIV-positive or negative, that they have a higher chance of destroying their health if they do not take precautions.

My mom (and God of course) has been a source of my strength throughout my coming to terms with my HIV status. She is one of the strongest people I know. While she remained, and remains to this day, a phenomenal woman, she taught me all the life lessons possible, including how to be a responsible man.

Curiously, while my mom is not extremely expressive with her emotions I seem to be overly expressive and sensitive. This past year was the first time I ever noticed the pain and sorrow within her. She never weakened, but I saw that some of her defenses had broken down. I never wanted to hurt my mom or cause her the stress I did, but I can't take back what happened. She is so strong, first having to deal with me telling her I am gay, and then that I have HIV.

One thing I will say is my mom loved me unconditionally and she has never given up on me. I understand now more than ever that even in the times I doubted it my mom never stopped loving me. She had to be stern and tough because if she hadn't, I wouldn't be as strong as I am now. I can finally appreciate that. Just because someone doesn't love you the way you want them to doesn't mean they don't love you!

My mom loved me more than I even loved myself. She loved me back into loving myself. Even with the complex relationship I had with my dad or my other life circumstances, my mom would assure me that she was there whenever I needed her to be. I am blessed to have her as my mom. My biggest pain came from causing my mother pain. So much that at our last Christmas I had to let her know how I felt. This is what I wrote to her along with a framed picture I gave her of me when I was a child.

Poetry

Just Look Into My Eyes
Just look into my eyes, so many stories to be told
Too much life lived for a 23 year old
I miss those times When I'd sit and play with my cars
And now life's got me bruised
And I'm still showing scars
I miss watching Smurfs in the morning
Or simply admiring you from afar
Made me want to replicate the person that you are
Look into my eyes
You'll see fear of the unknown
So many lessons I've yet to learn
Yet I appear to be full grown
Still hanging on
Afraid to stand on my own two
It's always good to know I can lean on you

Whether I'm smiling Or ready to cry
Living Or about to die
Strong Or feeling weak
Speechless Or available to speak
Young or grown Grey and old
My hearts in your hands
Is still what you hold
Look into my eyes
You'll see the struggle-Of the roads I've traveled down
Times you were right there Or nowhere around
I'm calling out But most times I'm not heard
So I ran out of hope Allowing myself not to say a word
I've done many things
Most I'd say I wouldn't-
That's not cool I lost control at a point
Didn't know what to do
I'm still trying to build
Trying to get back my stance Hoping to fix things
Before I don't have a chance
I don't know what's wrong with me
Whether I have long to live or soon to die
But remember me for the innocence
You used to see within my eyes
The times I'd be downstairs
Playing in the dirt
Always to myself
Seldom getting hurt
Or the times I'd ask to drink the pickle juice
Or when you taught me to tie my shoes because the
strings were always loose
Taught me to wash dishes
And I got water in the socket
All the memories I hold in my pocket
When your car got stolen I was so scared
Another new experience I was so unprepared

All the concerts Universal studios
And my infatuation with cars
You saw me through I didn't have my daddy But I
knew I had you
Look into my eyes-as they water
For tomorrow is not a guarantee
Hope you don't find yourself disappointed in me
I mean-I want you to look into my eyes
And not see someone crazy but still see me as your
1st born baby
Not a guy who's been raped or a homeless one that
almost overdosed on drugs
Someone that almost committed suicide because he
felt he lacked love & hugs
Someone that used to sell his time and body Just for
validation
One that's been broken hearted
Constant devastation
One that's never really been happy
Most times hating
His life is one that dates men that may never have a
wife
Someone that's been betrayed and played
Mistakes made may be dying of diabetes cancer,
maybe even AIDS
Someone that starves himself because he's dealing
with so much unhappiness and pain
Doesn't even realize he's doing it
Because it's become such a constant thing
Someone that loves God feels his purpose still stands
And regardless of what others may think
He's still a good man
I don't want to be judged just cherished while I'm here
I want to be loved completely
Loved sincere

I'd given it many tries failure-took control
But look into my eyes so you can see deep into my
soul I'm hurting
I'm crying I need a way out I'm stuck and out of luck
Is this what life's all about?
I'll keep hiding the pain
Way deep behind my eyes
To wake up the next morning
Presenting someone who really has on a disguise
I love You mom
Thanks for always being there.

I can't say I'm proud of many of the decisions I made in my life. I can't take back what's already done, so I am learning to just live and accept the mistakes I made. I'm trying to make the best of things, but when I think of those I love the most, I can't help but feel that I disappointed them. I'm actually kind of embarrassed. How am I supposed to tell the other people I love about what I have done and the hurt that I have caused? At one point I would have rather them believe I have a form of cancer or something. I think I had been dealing with everything pretty well up to the point where I thought about how they'd feel and how they'd react to me after my confession. After all it had taken me four days to build up the courage just to tell my mom.

I thank my mom endlessly for energizing me to just be strong and attempt to jump this hurdle. She told me not to let it get me stumped and she is totally right! I can't! My heart is still beating, so I got to still live but it doesn't mean my mind will stop taking the turns it does or my mind set stays normal. I'm scared and sometimes all I can think of is the worst. I just wish things could be the way they used to be. But in the meantime, I will have to keep expressing things day by day for each day is another journey and another road to travel down. God still has me, let's see what he does with me. Amen

CHAPTER 11
Butterfly Effect

The Butterfly Effect in humans is that of change and transitioning, the metamorphosis of being who and what we were created for is not always easy. It's actually quite challenging. The struggle is real. The struggle that life may bring is one thing, but making sense of it all is a whole other thing. I tend to struggle with myself, my identity, relationships and everything. I can't help but wonder if it is really possible for me to love and attain love the same way. Why is it so hard?

HIV...ugh! It's kinda like I have one strike against me from the get go. At least that's how it feels. It's so hard to be in a position where I'm obligated to be vulnerable and to reveal my status from the jump so they can decide if they want to reject me or if they're willing to take a chance. What kinda stuff is that? It's like each time I find I am interested in someone, it's a gamble of if he'll chance it or if he will say he's not willing.

If I don't say anything right away. I'm considered to be wrong for not sharing my status almost immediately, even if I protect myself and my partner always. Sometimes I think it's easier to be alone but loneliness is the other side of that coin.

Rejection now is the norm. I can't say it helps my esteem and of course other people aren't considerate enough to keep the information to themselves. People will share your business, no matter how personal, like they do a pack of gum. Always being expected to leave your life at the disposal of other people who don't even value themselves seems crazy. You can't expect them to value your business if they don't value their own. And rejection can appear at so many levels of relationships.

I used to struggle with accepting the reality of my status. I used to think that if I didn't tell people, that it wouldn't be as much of a reality, but not talking about it doesn't change anything. The struggle, it turns out, is all in my mind. What is it I am so afraid of? Most times it's other people's perception and opinions, but why is it I find that to be so significant? I find the struggle of acceptance is usually based on the lack of awareness of someone else, and that caused me to limit myself and struggle with my truth.

I'm constantly battling, constantly fighting, constantly at war but even the strongest soldiers gotta rest sometimes. It's not easy trying to remain sane and intact after being exposed to the harsh realities of illness and rejection. In fact I'm surprised I'm still here and haven't given up yet. There are still times I cry while I pretend to be someone strong. I hide the pain and only cry behind closed doors. They say never show your tears. Never show your weaknesses. But if you're a weakened soul always in pain, how can it not show?

Before I left for Los Angeles and the resources available there I was staying at my parents' house. I must say it was awkward. Though my mom was being supportive throughout this new ordeal, she was the only one who knew what was going on, so on the other end, I looked like a grown ass man sitting up in the house not contributing or paying bills, and that wasn't gonna cut it.

Have you ever been somewhere that you had to be because you had nowhere else to go, but you also knew you weren't wanted where you were staying? Well, that was my situation. Just some tension that couldn't be ignored. I found that I was consistently getting into it with my dad, always disappointing my mom. I just couldn't do anything right. I found myself getting reprimanded and in trouble so often that it didn't even surprise me anymore. I started feeling miserable. I began gaining resentment and that wasn't a healthy situation. I had to grow up. I expected my parents to feed and support me because I was felt sorry for myself and my situation. That wasn't my intention, but that's what it had become.

When I left for L.A. was one of the first times I truly had to step out on faith and see where life would lead me. God is something else. Though I knew He existed, I didn't really know I had a direct connection to him at this point, so I believed in Him but not fully. I didn't know if He really knew me or heard my prayers, but they somehow got to Him. Kinda like Monica. I've met her five times, and each time there was something in the way she looked at me that told me she remembered seeing me and meeting me, but may not have remembered where. So we have a connection, but it may not quite be as direct as I would like. (Maybe that example was a stretch ... but you get it.) This is one serious journey and I'm doin' my best to try to remain strong, to keep standing and to keep going. But slowly my legs are weakening and I wanna take a seat. It's crazy.

Overall, it feels like nobody truly knows or understands how I'm feeling inside or out. Nobody knows how depressing it is to have to take the medicine I take two times a day every day. It's a constant reminder saying, "Hey, by the way you are HIV-positive in case you forgot." It's like having to relive it each day, and people have the nerve to say you can still live a normal life. Yea, okay, a normal life that consists of pills and side-effects. They never told me how nauseous the medicine would make me feel. And this is supposed to excite me about taking the pills more the next day? Yeah right. I don't like this.

Nobody understands the constant fear that my illness will become worse and bring me down to the state of the next possible diagnosis of AIDS. I mean I'm not the only person with this condition, but I'm the only person that I know of all the people I know in my world. In my close circle nobody knows or understands. They don't understand how it feels to be discouraged about life, love or the hopes of finding love because people aren't necessarily gonna want to date me if they find out I have HIV.

I already felt undesirable, but now I feel disgusting and nobody ever approaches me or shows interest in me. Why? Even if they did, it's because they don't know what I have. Would someone want to put up with the things my life now entails? It's hard to remain optimistic. It's hard to keep smiling. It's hard to wake up each day. It's hard to have to live a life you hate. It's hard not feeling wanted and loved or appreciated when going through such hard times. I just wanna be happy! I just wanna be free. I just want someone to love me for me. Will I ever get that? Do I deserve what I seek? Is anyone listening? Can anyone hear what I speak?

Poetry

Prisoner of Circumstance
Incarcerated by my emotions
Societies got me chained
My soul's losing its devotion
And it's driving me insane
My hearts restrained behind bars
It's probably why love can't get through
Dearest circumstance I'm a prisoner of you
All these brick walls built with purpose of security
But now they're closing in on me
And being used against me
Circumstances got me guarded
And surrounded by those that couldn't care less
How could these odds be beat?
With a broken heart in my chest
Distorted verbalizations
One to always be misunderstood
A prisoner of circumstance
No way I'd even be free if I could
Lifetime prisoner circumstance, I have no parole
Some things you can change
Others you just can't control
There's no escaping
No matter how deep the hole
I'm now a prisoner of life
Losing sense of my soul
Trying to get it back

Trying to grasp the essence of strength
But my circumstances restrained me to the fullest
extent
I'm waiting on a bonds man
I'm waiting to put up bail
Before this prisoner of circumstance does his time in
hell.

As I came to grips with my diagnosis I endured some of the most difficult times in my life. I felt like I was kinda forced to experience life unprepared. I mean, I had a good upbringing, but I was not shown the different things I would need to understand and navigate through it. I didn't understand why I felt unloved and so eagerly longed to feel it, especially from a man. I didn't know why I was always treated like I was the enemy when I tried to be completely loving, helpful and supportive.

It's like I spent a majority of my life seeking to be validated and accepted, but I could never make everyone happy. I always felt like a failure. I struggled with my self-esteem. I didn't know who I was nor did I truly love anything I saw when I looked into the mirror. It didn't help that I felt as if no one else really loved me, so it made me believe I was not loveable. A lot of these emotions came about as I went through life experiences and didn't feel I had support or resources to guide me through. I found out in time that these were all the key moments that helped mold me into the person I have become.

After finding out I was HIV positive, I also found myself homeless for the second time in my life. After

MAP helped me get medical services and got me situated with a dosage regimen, they helped me find options for living. I was able to move into a Transitional Living Home (TLH) sponsored by the Gay and Lesbian Center in Hollywood. I remember before getting into this program, I had a meeting at MAP to do the paperwork. I was nervous. I was living with a friend but as soon as we completed the paperwork I had until the end of the day to get all of my stuff and move into the program. I was nervous because it was happening so fast.

The transitional living program was a great thing for me. My friend who allowed me to live with him spoke about how this might help me get to where I eventually wanted to go. I was scared. I feared the unknown, but knowing that I had his support made me feel that things would be okay. He dropped me off and I felt like I was turning a page and opening up a new chapter of my life. Saying goodbye was so nerve wrecking for me.

The TLH place was huge! By the look of the outside, it was a bit intimidating. I went in and I was introduced to the staff. They showed me my room. This was gonna be a different environment. Rooms were shared four people to a room. There were a total of six rooms. Every room had two bunk beds, and each person had their own dresser and a locker. A thin closet had a combination lock on the outside so that you could lock your private stuff away. The staff had your combination just in case they needed to check for weapons or drugs and they could search whenever they wanted.

In this residence program, there was a TV room, where we could watch TV shows and movies and we could also request to block out certain times if we wanted to watch certain shows or whatever. There was a shelf of books for those who enjoyed reading, there was a computer room where we were allowed to look for jobs and there were two hours a day where people would be able to go on Myspace (before Facebook was popular) or whatever to interact freely. Of course the staff monitored the activities 'cause many of the kids would start browsing sites that were inappropriate.

There was also a dining room area, kitchen, and laundry room. The laundry room was great 'cause they provided us with laundry detergent to wash our clothes, they also provided us with hygiene products if we needed them, and best of all, they provided us three meals a day. I remember we had a cook, and she was such a beautiful person. Her heart was golden and she truly loved and cherished the kids in the program. She believed in God and prayed for a lot of us from time to time which to me was very comforting. There was even a clothing closet for anyone who needed clothes. This is where I began building my wardrobe. My new living arrangement seemed like a very community based version MTV's *The Real World* and it was amazing that such programs existed for young HIV-positive folks. Before this I had no idea.

One thing I came to realize is that it had always been difficult for me to hold down a job, because I never had a stable place to lay my head. Before this place, I didn't know where I would be from day to day. I was truly in a transition to more responsibility because once I got into this program, and I felt as if I had a stable place to live day to day. I became motivated to look for work once again 'cause I finally didn't have to worry about where I was going to be staying each night. When in survival mode, my priorities were eating, a safe place to sleep and a safe place to keep the stuff I do own. Now those three things weren't a concern for me.

It took me just two weeks to find myself a job. I initially got hired at Banana Republic which was down the street from where my new home was. A week after that, I landed my second job at Jerry's Famous Deli in Studio City. Life was truly starting to look up for me. The requirements for the program were that each person had to be working or going to school. We also had to make monthly deposits (kinda like rent) in which we deposited 70% of whatever our income was. The other 30% was for whatever we chose to use it for (phone bills, extracurricular activities, etc.). Actually, we didn't need for much else.

Another requirement was that we met with a case manager once a week and also a therapist once a week. The case managers were pretty much only making sure we followed the rules and were making our deposits. I remember one time I had to manipulate the rules a bit. Though they required we work and/or go to school, everyone was still given a curfew. I was expected to be in no later than 8:00 PM. The longer you are there and following rules the more they extend out the curfew. But since I had two jobs I had to find a loophole in the system.

I was working at Banana Republic from 7:00 AM to1:00 PM and then I worked at Jerry's Deli on the graveyard shift. So I had to be there from 9:00 PM to

5:00 AM. Sometimes I would start earlier at 7:00 PM to get in more hours. This would give me enough time to get home, change for work and get to Jerry's by 7:00. I would rest in between jobs. This was a conflict for a case manager because he said I had to quit the graveyard job because of my curfew. I had a very interesting conversation with him. I pointed out that there were no written rules stating that there were only certain types of jobs we could accept. It just stated that we had to have one. I pointed out how difficult it was to get a job and that if I quit my second job, it would only mean that the program was not really interested in in our progress and development because making me quit wouldn't allow me to develop the skills or build up the cash necessary to get out of my current situation. I asked him, "Do you want me to quit the job that you forced me to go find? That makes no sense to me and I find it to be quite frustrating." I added on a few extra points, and dramatics, and I got my way.

This was my way of getting out of the house when I wanted to go out or have fun. I had to leave at the same time I would for work, and return at the usual time as well. It was kinda like I made my own rules with the curfew. I also made sure I did my required weekly chore on time so that my time out of the home would not be questioned.

When it came to the "therapist" they assigned to me he turned out to be a fool who couldn't care less about me. It only took me two sessions to call him out on it. I said, "You aren't even listening to me. What's the point of me coming to see you from week to week?" He tried to deny it so I asked him, "Okay then repeat to me what I was just talking to you about if you were listening." He couldn't. I then went to my case manager and told him, "If I am required to see a therapist once a week, I should be able to find one who cares about me and who could help me evolve. I want the opportunity to find my own therapist." He allowed me the opportunity to and I went back to MAP to get counseling from them. I was making things happen up in this place, and I was making them work to my benefit. My self-esteem was improving.

I definitely had some interesting experiences while I was in TLH program. There were kids in the program would try to commit suicide. There were others had mental health issues and this was my first time seeing how real mental health issues effected young people. Some young people were seeking to find themselves through Drag, some by starting to take hormones to transition to becoming the opposite gender, and there were some who were seriously battling drugs and alcohol addictions. There were so many layers to the challenges young people my age were experiencing. I kinda looked at it like a hospital. We were all in need of help, healing, revitalization, something. We needed to be made better. We needed help. The sad thing was to see that some weren't ready or willing to do their part to make it a success. The other part was that many of the staff people didn't care much about the clients and did not provide the proper support or tools the young people needed to progress.

This is when I realized my passion for helping

others that were going through some of the things I had. I began volunteering at MAP and providing Peer Counseling to the other clients in the TLH program. I remember there was a guy who worked there, Chris D., and he was the one guy who was supportive, encouraging and who always showed he cared. There were not many straight dudes that showed this level of compassion for young black gay kids, but he said he knew I was destined for greatness, and he made my experience of living there bearable. Whenever I needed solitude to maintain my peace of mind, he would allow me to lock myself in a storage room with my head phones and my music and notebook. I would write for hours and hours. I think I did some of my best writing in that storage room because I had so much emotion to sort out.

I thank God for Chris D. He was like a guardian angel. He would tell me I was going to be okay when I didn't think I would be. Having a person there to encourage you when you feel you are at your lowest point in your life is such a blessing. It shows that God will never leave you and that he will use his angels to reach you in the places that you may not think He can find you. God needs you to know you will be protected no matter what your situation may look like. I stayed in this program for eight months until I turned 24 years old. That's when the program ended for me.

You know what? After the love, sorrow, pain and weakness I experienced from being raped as an eighth grader to the time that I was 24 and on the precipice of going out truly on my own, I gained strength. God is good. I found myself depressed sitting there dwelling on what I thought would be my new horrible reality, my new life, my new problem, my new trials and tribulations about my new awareness, new diagnosis, new disease but instead I found new faith! I found new strength, new hope, new love, new pride, new belief, new encouragement, brand new positivity and a whole new appreciation for living despite what had happened to me.

I made the mistake of claiming HIV, of calling it a new addition in my life when in reality it's not even a fraction of who I am or what I'll be. I no longer will even speak it as a reality that effects who I am. Of course I'll be wise and take the necessary precautions to keep myself and other safe and to make my situation as easy and great as possible.

I admit HIV may have gotten me down at first, and it may have depressed me temporarily. But had I failed to look to God or to simply acknowledge how good He's been and all that He constantly does for me. I know in my heart He won't stop now. He never will. He loves me far too much to ever leave or forsake me. And I will never overlook that aspect of my reality again.

I just want to thank God for giving me the incredible insight that He's given me. I vow to look at life in the best and most positive forms possible. I love you Lord. I swear my life has changed. I'll do what it takes to insure it's for the better benefit of you and to fulfill the destiny you seek for me. Lord, you are my strength. Some things will kill you if you allow them to, but Lord I am your servant and I ain't goin' nowhere.

I know the situation is crazy. It is still hard for me to grasp but I know I'm gonna be fine because of you Lord. So don't think otherwise, get that out of your mind. I'm still doing what I gotta do. Staying alive so I can spend more time with you on Earth. It ain't easy I'll never front and say it is. So each time I take the medication that gives me more chance to survive I ain't goin nowhere, I'm staying alive.

Poetry

Who Doesn't Get Scared?

Who doesn't get scared?
Who doesn't cry?
I may do it a little more often
But that doesn't mean goodbye.
You amaze me how within a short time
You can take me to a whole new life.
Without going any place it amazes me how I'm happy and smile
Each time I see your face
It amazes me the comfort
I'm compelled to love the life that remains
When other times I'm alone and feel I'm going insane
In constant pain
But won't be distorted by the rain
Still got life to live so much more to gain
So brother, best-friend, one
That I share love and care
Keep in mind- and never forget
I ain't goin nowhere, I'm gonna be all right!
I still got goals to reach, money to make, things to accomplish, Monica to work with
So much more to do
So much more success to achieve

Much more life to live!

I have found the most vital component of healing is forgiveness. I needed the Lord to transform me into the man he wanted me to be. I don't wanna continue to dwell on past misery and look at the sunshine like it wasn't meant for me. Sometimes I get a sudden chill and I can't seem to feel the warmth even though the clear sky is so beautiful and surreal. Sometimes the cloud rotation resembles the way my emotions shift. I'm trying to love as one of God's greatest gifts. But how do I show my appreciation? By being mean or taking others for granted? That is not the way. I am very choosey about who I associate with but I can't repair my life single handedly. I think better of it by asking, "Who am I to be picky?" Perfection is far from what I represent. I am still learning to love myself and I still need the Lord's understanding and guidance to get to a life that's pure. I feel I've advanced and grown in ways but in many ways I'm still unsure. Am I even worthy of all the blessings God has given while I'm still trying to find my purpose and even my motivation for living? Each time I rise up I find myself bringing me back down. I can't believe the person I've become. I don't even like thinking I'm better than others. It's okay to hold my head high but not above all others. So I'm sorry to everyone I've hurt and to God who I'm striving to meet one day in the heavenly sky. Please forgive me Lord for all that I've done. Change me and mold me to become the man I should be.

Poetry

I'm Sorry *(one of my favorites by Anonymous)*

I just wanna say I'm sorry
For all those I may have made cry
I'm seeking to find clarity Amongst You and I
I'm sorry if I ever was mean to you
Sorry if I caused you hurt
Sorry if I ever made you feel As if I dropped you in the
dirt
Sorry if I ever ignored you
Sorry if ever a promise was broke
Sorry if I ever saw you And I forgot to respond as you
spoke
Sorry if I ever snapped at you
Sorry if I made you mad
The thing is I can't take back those things
And I'm sorry- I feel bad
Sorry if I was UN-logical
Sorry if I was ever unfair
Sorry if you needed me
And I just wasn't there
Sorry if you ever called on me
But I would just misunderstand
Sorry if you ever reached out for me
But I didn't reach out my hand.
Sorry if I ever laughed at you
Sorry if I made fun
Sorry if I never gave you a chance before the
opportunity even begun
I'm so sorry if I ever led you on
So sorry if I've ever done you wrong
Sorry if you ever loved me and I didn't know how to
love you back
Sorry if you ever cared for me when compassion was
what I lacked
Sorry if I've had a negative impact in your life
If only the time I could erase

Then I wouldn't have to say I'm sorry
And there'll be a smile upon your face
I'm sorry you had to meet me
I'm sorry that there were feelings you had to
overcome
Sorry I didn't know better I feel so damn dumb
I'm sorry if you hate me
Sorry if you wish I were dead I never meant to hurt
anyone
So I'm saying sorry instead
I'm hoping you'd forgive me
If not...hey I did say I was sorry
There's not much more I can say
May God always bless you and may you get all that
you pursue
But if you get nothing else from this
Realize-I'm saying I'm sorry to you.
But I Still Love You
Broke down walls
That'll never be rebuilt
Stayed with me cause you were feeling guilt
Walked out the door Didn't even close it behind
Expected it to stay open
Are you out of your damn mind?
Gave you all of me When I didn't hardly have anything
left
And that quick-you took my heart And tore it out of my
chest
But I still love you even though another brother's
love's exceeding mine
I got my head up and I'll be just fine
There's no denying You had me hatin' you for about a
cool 24 Hours
Passing-the pain grew, Made me resent you more
You made a mockery of my love, of my life, and want

another stab at it
I don't have much heart left don't think I could let you
have it
But I still Love you.
Over 40 people you had me on the side
Each word you would speak Turned out to be a lie
But I remained loyal
Tried so hard to believe that it was only a phase
And that your bads and wrongs would soon leave
Who was I foolin'? Myself.
Cause in the end that's all I had You didn't love me, or
even care, didn't even feel bad
All the time, money, miles invested into this
Thinking I found love and a life full of bliss
What did I miss? Must've been reality 'cause when I
looked again you were never beside me You got what
you wanted
And left my heart in the sand
Didn't even try to explain yourself
Didn't care to help me understand
It took a while to get over it
And it seems a part of you will always live with me
Something everlasting
Some call it HIV
But I still Love you
I lived off of promises
And broken dreams
And the men in my life
Were never what they seemed
I'm learning from my mistakes
But am I learning too late I still love you
Even though you helped determine my mind-state
I gave you my heart, my soul, I gave you everything
I was always what you wanted me to be
You were my king

So much passion, so sensational I just knew it was a
fresh start
Who would've known you'd be one to step over my
heart?
I mean the way you held me
The things you said made me feel so complete
The only to bring a tear to my eyes
From knocking me off of my feet
Another defeat the way you'd retreat
When you crossed my path
After that night I couldn't add up the aftermath
But you wouldn't acknowledge me
Speak, call, or write at all
What changed? I thought I wasn't the only one to fall
Standing tall
Alone, daydreaming and you just laughing and
carrying on
Not reaching you took my heart into another zone
It took me forever to understand I still take offense
How could you utilize my body?
But forsake me ever since
All the letters you gave no response, all the calls-no
return
I'd even say hi just to be ignored when will I ever
learn?
You meant so much to me even though I didn't mean
shit to you
But after all the tears, heartache, pain and depression
I have to say
I still love you
We had a love so perfect
Something only God can make
After months of time and effort I realized it was all a
fake
Yeah you did like me

But weren't ready to commit
Why did you wait until I got attached before you told
me this shit
You were my partner, my angel, my lover, truly my
right hand
There through all the hard times, you were such a
good man
You taught me to cook
Made sacrifices did your 50%
But when I said let's make it official
You were running out the fence
No hard feelings
At least you showed me you cared
I'd rather you run than pretend to be prepared
Now I see you it kinda hurts
Watching you love another man
Were there things he do that I just never can?
Left me alone I can say we were just at a bad state in
time
So the reality is I know you'd never be mine!
But I still love you!

CHAPTER 12
Hope

HOPE: Having an Optimistic Perspective Every time. It's really hard to maintain a sense of hope sometimes in life when you may feel as if things are moving more toward a hopeless outcome. Hope still believes in chance and opportunity in spite of what life presents. My hope for love and everlasting relationships seems to waiver now and not be what it once was. I am not sure what exactly I believe in these days. What I do know is that life is truly what I make it and with all the different things I've been through and have overcome, I know that I will be all right. I also know that I can truly get through anything, because God has already revealed to me that I can get through the very things I thought would kill me.

Who would have thought that I would live the life that I have and still have a great heart and positive mind? I am fortunate that my attempts to end my life were not successful. That is the only failure I would claim. I am glad I failed at interrupting my purpose and trying to destroy the great impact I am meant to make in this world.

You've heard the saying "Be careful what you ask for." Well, I was begging and pleading for companionship and to not be alone, but I was not specific in what I sought, and I was given an option that was not the one meant for me to take. I say not meant, but maybe it was because I don't have any regrets or feel like my journey was a mistake. I believe that I was expected to go through the things I have to share the things I did, to help the people I will. Truth is, I am HIV-positive and I am making something greater of my life and being more than just my "HIV circumstance."

It's sad to say but I am not sure what my purpose would be if I hadn't encountered what I have to ignite the things that it did. After going through the levels of complication striving to find access to resources and services necessary to maintain a healthy lifestyle, I came to a clearer vision of what I can contribute to this world. I feel that God has created me to serve and servitude is where I find most of my blessings results from. He will not put more upon us than we can bear.

Living with HIV is a life change, though many would say life is not much different. I would say that a life change is actually something people should shift and change whether they are negative or HIV-positive. Some of those changes are simply eating better, meditation, eliminating stress, exercise, and being more conscious of how life is lived. Extra precaution needs to be taken around protecting sexual partners (where any and everyone should be using protection), and each partner should be tested to determine his HIV status. It's not always easy, so I make it a point to talk to my friends and peers about ways that this discussion can happen and to negotiate having safe and protected sex even though in the heat of the moment, it's not always easy.

After my experience, I want to make sure I position myself to provide the information for people that I felt I wasn't provided or that wasn't easy for me to come by. I want to prevent people from having to go through some of the things I had to. I truly do have Hope for a better world, and I believe it starts with each individual.

It took me just a while to realize that HIV wasn't a death sentence and that I can still actively live a fulfilling life with this disease as long as I do what it takes to take care of myself. My best friend always gets me to work out, because he knows I would much rather sit up in the local restaurant and work the waiter out by having him run back and forth to bring me some food. I began volunteering at a local agency called In The Meantime Men's group in Los Angeles, and it allowed me the opportunity of fellowship and being around other Black Gay Men. I feel as though I am finally gaining a sense of who I was meant to be in my community.

I have also learned not to expect too much from other people, especially if I am not expecting it from myself! I have to stop expecting the world to cater to me. I have to be a go-getter and go for what I want or need in my life. My own action is the only thing I can expect because it is the only thing I have control over. It doesn't help when I look at examples of some of the relationship around me that they never appear to be that great or worth it! So maybe I am just a hopeless romantic when it comes to love.

Smile
Early in the morning it seems I just can't make it out of bed I just got this feeling
Can't get those thoughts up out my head
I lay there for a minute I have to look around
'Cause last night I swear you were right there
Maintaining your throne and crown

But this morning I reach around me I even find myself
calling your name
Was it all a dream?
Are these emotions apart of the game?
Can't be-because I see the imprints you left from the
night before
You wrote all over my heart; my soul and even
opened up new doors
Exposing me to places I no longer thought were in
reach I allowed you access to my love
But I needed To practice what I preached
You loved me a lot
And I truly loved you too
And as far as I'm concerned
My love will never be through I don't know what to do
Laugh, daydream, smile or cry 'cause truly in my mind
I thought we'd said goodbye
But now I open my eyes
Still laying here in bed
All of a sudden rejuvenated
Because of the life that we have ahead
I jump up like I was by a trampoline and say thank
God for love and allowing me to know what it means
I turn on my radio
It seems every song is sung for you
I find your imaging In everything I do
Wash my face, I smile 'cause I imagine us on the
beach
Stretch my arms; I smile because I feel we are finally
back in reach
Brush my teeth, I smile because you make me just
want to
Shower, smile 'cause of the many things I know we'd
do
Do my hair, smile 'cause I imagine you next to me

doing your own
The phone rings, I smile I imagine it's you on the
phone
Doing my push-ups, I smile 'cause for you I'm trying
to get a tight look in the mirror
I smile 'cause today I'm feeling right!
Then I pause for a moment
Just a day before I wouldn't even grin I thought I lost
love thought we'd never talk again
So glad we got to talk so glad we could reconnect
And this time our relationship I will protect
Put on my clothes, I smile 'cause I imagine you taking
them off
Walk through the house, I smile I imagine we had us a
two-bedroom with a loft
I walk outside, I smile 'cause the shine of the sun is
bright
So I smile 'cause for a change I know I'll be all right!

CHAPTER 13
Acceptance

It took me years but I finally realized that in order to be accepted, I must accept myself. I question even now how relevant it is to be accepted by others. It seems that all that acceptance and flattery from others is just the stuff that feeds our egos. If I live in purpose, treating people well and living happily does their acceptance of me even matter?

Depending on who we are seeking it from, acceptance can be an overrated thing that, honestly, many will never even get. You can never be accepted by everyone so you must accept yourself instead. Living in your Truth and being okay with who you were created to be sounds simple but is the most you can do. My ability to stand firm regardless of what people may say or think about me is crucial. The moment I was able to share my status and openly say that I'm HIV-positive was the moment I felt the chains fall away. I knew I didn't care what people thought anymore. Finally, their judgment could not change my reality or my perspective on life.

Poetry

I Am a Prostitute for Love
Prostitute, only selling my soul for emotional gain
In hopes that it'll relieve me
Of all this pain I'm insane
Always available and willing to please
Hoping to find love

And that the heartache will cease
But who am I foolin' I'm a fool in a bad situation
Deceived and used to believe
There'll be some compensation when devastation takes over
The more I find myself used allowing my heart to be controlled and my spirit abused
Always refused-when love is what I try to give
It's like I'm a prostitute and this ain't no way to live
In the end all I see are condom wrappers on the floor
To be disposed of, like me
Thinking there was passion
Yet I still feel so empty
This ain't me nor how I want to be
Emotional prostitution ain't the thing for me.
I'm allowing you access, pure opportunity to become one and connected to me
I'm allowing you to strip me of insecurities
Along with my doubts and pride
I'll allow you to the closed-up places I've held deep inside
I'll allow you the security code
Therefore I won't be alarmed
But one thing I ask you to grant me
Is respect and promise to do me no harm
I'll allow you to be my lover
I'll allow you to be my friend
Just know that I'm being cautious 'cause my heart didn't completely mend
I wanna trust you; I wanna love you and start our forever today
But I need you to allow me To know you completely
I need the honesty, loyalty and faithfulness too
Respect me promise me that you'll be there
So as my clothes hit the floor

You stripped away all others
There's no more holding back
We now are lovers
Don't let me down!
I gain tranquility from your embrace
I gain security by seeing your face
I gain joy as I put back on my shirt
I gain assurance that you won't provide hurt
I gain new perspective
Smile as I put on my shoes
Find myself trembling as we proclaim 'I love you'
Wow! This is how it feels to be loved
I gain knowledge and understanding as our passion
burns
Did I finally earn back all that I gave?
Is this what I waited for?
Is this why I live?
To be truly and sincerely loved, to the highest extent
possible
I thank God for this chance
So meaningful and heaven sent
I've finally become who I am supposed to be
Again I thank God for sending true love to me
Got me goin' out of my head
How will I ever find the words
How would we stand face to face?
When deep within I feel such a disgrace
You respected me
That's something I don't wanna lose
Lack of intelligence and wisdom I failed to use
See now it started back like L.L.
I needed love
Tried to get it by sex sometimes without "the Glove"
What was I thinking of?
But now I know better

A little too late
Now I go by three letters
It's destroying me I think
I'm just afraid to face the fact
That I lost my self-control
Lost something I'll never get back
My life, all the strife I went through to make it to "me"
Now I'll probably never understand what all I can be
I can't stop living still much life for me to live
But when it comes to telling you I have no words to
lend or give
You're so significant all others- I don't give a damn
You're like the only person in this world who took time
out to get to know who I am
Damn, damn, damn... I ain't trying to be judged
They say it's all in my head but the realness ain't
budged
Will you change on me?
Will you care even less?
Cause so far in life I have been truly blessed
With a true friend, a good man
Together we went through a lot and truly I'd have to
say you're all that I've got
I'm just goin' out of my head I'm afraid things will shift
When you find out what I got
I think my strength and courage need a lift
If I could change the cards that were dealt to me
I would change my whole destiny
I'd face a new reality but I should just deal
There's power in wisdom..... power in knowledge.....
Power in our words, actions and thoughts
We really hold the power over our lives, our hearts,
happiness and destiny
The question is what will you do with that Power?

CHAPTER 14
Closure

What happens after someone has finally come to terms with the life they were given? The cards that they were dealt? The responsibilities of their purpose? We must embrace, endure, adjust, reflect and continue. There's nothing we can do to change life, so as opposed to complaining about it, we must find a way to deal.

Fortunately, I took my experience and made something positive out of it. I am now in a position where I work in the community I come from, and I am able to provide the services I felt once were lacking when I sought them. I am able to connect with individuals who have always felt ignored or over looked. I am able to relate about the things that I had been through and that I've overcome. I am now able to navigate others through systems that I had to figure out on my own. It wasn't easy and I must admit it was quite discouraging.

I am now helping people access the services and resources that I once needed. It's so amazing how God brought me through ... so I can help a few. It's sometimes difficult helping someone else when we are still trying to figure things out for ourselves but I somehow learned to manage the art of it. It also speaks to the fact that everything happens for a reason. If I hadn't endured the things I had, I wouldn't be doing this kind of work. If I weren't doing this kind of work, I am not even too sure what I would be doing. It's all a part of my purpose.

Of all the things, the most interesting thing for me was learning to navigate through this new journey of my life. Sometimes we find that the journey seems a bit rougher when we have no one to blame, or who can share the responsibility of what happened or what was ahead. But for me, I found that what was most challenging for me was not feeling that I had closure with the person I once dated who introduced this virus to me.

I thought I had completely forgiven him but for some reason deep inside I still harbored a lot of resentment and anger but most of my anger, bitterness, pain and hurt came from trying to understand why this had happened to me. I didn't understand how someone could be so heartless, when I just needed to use my heartless, and understand that not everyone will stick by the words they say by following it up in actions. Lesson learned. I held a serious grudge against him for a long time, but as time went on, I recognized much clearer what my purpose was.

I also know that at the time I may not have understood things or their reasons but soon enough it all began to make sense. I also recognized that if I hadn't been through the things I had, I wouldn't be the person I am. I had to forgive myself, and then forgive him as well. I had to stop putting all the blame on him and also take responsibility for my own actions and my role in the situation.

Whether I was aware and educated or not, I still allowed myself to be in a situation that I may not have been ready for, all in the search to feel loved, wanted and validated. I chose not to use protection with him. I chose to trust someone else more than my own instincts.

It's funny how the very thing that we think will fill us up and make us whole becomes the thing that leaves us feeling empty and unfulfilled. Many times it's because we are seeking it within another human being, in a way that's designed to fail, and we aren't looking to the one that we should, the One who created us.

Forgiveness is key. I didn't know how to forgive myself because I didn't love myself and I felt as if it was punishment for my existence, not a repercussion of my actions. I didn't get why I always ended up hurt whenever it came to matters of my heart. Every time I trusted or let someone in, I ended up hurting.

Besides myself, I had to forgive the person who I viewed as an enemy, my downfall and the reason I would no longer live what I thought was considered a normative life anymore. The more grudges that we hold onto, the less hands we have to grab hold of the new blessings that will come into your life. I could not go back and change this situation, so I had to ask myself what will I make of my life now? I felt because of him, everything had to change.

I didn't think I would ever find someone to love me or that would want to be with me now that I am HIV Positive. It was quite devastating for me and I told myself I would never forgive him for doing this to me. As I grew up, I realized the only things that happen sometimes are the things that we allow to happen. I had to take responsibility and forgive myself, and also forgive him. I needed to be free. I was imprisoned and I was choosing to stay behind the bars when the cell had been opened for me to walk out when I was ready to do so. I had some healing to do, some revealing to do, some conversations with God that needed to take place, and tears that still needed to fall down my face in order for me to be able to take a few steps forward.

It wasn't long after I finally had that conversation with God and stated aloud that I forgive Him and him. Him (God) because I blamed Him for so long and accused Him of not loving me because I didn't think He would allow me to go through this if He truly did. I learned so much when I stopped assuming and started to pay attention to the message. I not only forgave God, but I had to ask Him for forgiveness. I know He understands me and knew it was no ill intent, but I had to clear the air.

Then I had to forgive the one that infected me. I had to let my hate go and loosen the chains that bound me to him. That kept giving him power in my life when he was no longer a part of it. The way God does things is kinda funny sometimes. I remember one day I was taking a client to get housing in the downtown area, down the street from what is commonly known as skid row, and I happened to see the person who gave me HIV, the very person who I was working so long to forgive.

When I saw him, I didn't feel the anger that 'this is the person who hurt me,' or 'this is the person who infected me.' I just felt sorrow and empathy for him. Here I am, a person that had the ability to take the cards I was dealt and make them work for me, and now I see this man after eight years and he's on skid row, looking as if he has not had a hot meal in months, looking as if his only motivation was to find his next hit. Here he was living on the street.

To look into a person's eyes that you once looked at with passion and hope for an everlasting union and to see that their spirit was dead and their hope evaporated, it made me want to cry. I thanked God for the ability to step outside of myself to look at the bigger picture.

He approached me and spoke, "Hey, how you been stranger? I haven't seen you in a while, you look great." I couldn't even force a smile, I was so concerned. I said "Thank you. It truly has been a while. I hope everything is all right for you. You know if you ever need assistance there are resources. Please know that the place I now work can provide assistance." I gave him a business card said "take care of yourself," and solemnly walked away.

It actually hurt me more to see that this is what had become of him. It hurt me more than the things that I allowed to be done to me. Never kick someone when they're down. I asked for God to bless him. The encounter spoke to me of the importance of forgiveness. God will deal, handle and manage all things. Most things are beyond our control. The beauty of turning what is meant to hurt, scar, damage or distract us from our purpose and instead to become empowered by it, to use it as a tool to bless other people and help them find God as a result is an awe inspiring thing. In that one fateful moment I was seized by love. I vow to never let go.

~~End~~

ABOUT THE AUTHOR: Greg Wilson, 33, is the Deputy Director of REACH LA (since 2007) a youth based organization in Los Angeles, CA. that focuses on serving young African American/Latino MSM in Los Angeles County. Before working at REACH LA, he worked at In The Meantime Men's Group for 3 years as a Health Educator/Program Coordinator. After working in the HIV/AIDS field for over 10 years, Greg's passion is evident and he has been recognized nationally for his efforts toward leadership development, job preparation and working closely with under-served populations such as the House and Ballroom Community.

Through the Ovahness program, which includes the Ovahness Ball, Greg reaches hundreds of youth each year. Greg finds his role and position as an opportunity and platform to connect/direct youth with whom he's built a strong relationship to the services and resources they need. Greg utilizes his expertise and experience to best serve the community he is passionate about by providing intense (Mental Health) counseling, mentorship, help in setting life-goals, encouraging HIV Testing and education, linkage into health care services and more. It's no wonder the community is now becoming more aware and taking control of their status, this epidemic and their lives.

Greg's efforts are expanded through his facilitation of life skill workshops, by addressing self-esteem concerns that are often overlooked, and helping develop strategies for other agencies to strengthen the leadership component of their programs. Greg's heart is shown through his effective work and endless efforts. Greg's hope is that this book will speak from the perspective of some of the youth that have felt for so long that they've had no voice, felt misunderstood, and who have overcome many struggles they weren't expected to survive. This book will be used as a tool of empowerment and will add to his effort to connect with the community on a deeper level. Greg is surely a trailblazer who commits his life to the betterment of his people, his community and this world.

Thank You

(To include but not limited to, and in no particular order)ALL of my friends, family, associates, inspirations, motivations, mentors, influences, acquaintances, peers, co-workers, collaborative partners. My House and Ballroom Family, Ovahness Leaders & Family, REACH LA (volunteers and staff), ITMT (and staff), APLA (and staff), CHLA (and staff),BAI (and staff), BTAN LA, Magic Johnson Foundation.God... It's finally done! You have been working through me for years to develop this work, that will hopefully impact lives, shift mindsets and provide hope. Love is the key to all things, and I had shared this perspective and story from a loving place. God knows what He is doing through me, and I trust that it will align with what His purpose for me is. I thank God for never letting me go or giving up on me, allowing me to gain strength and knowledge through my experiences as opposed to be over come by them. I am so blessed and grateful, and I look forward to what you have next in store for me Lord.Mom, I thank you for always having my back and never failing to be there throughout this journey. Marquez, you are my greatest inspiration. Tobaise Brookins, I thank you for being a true example of a man and taking the time to mentor me and helping me recognize my purpose in life. Most importantly, you've helped me build and develop my relationship with God, and also broke down the things I didn't understand, and I am blessed and grateful for the impact you have made in my life! Thank You! Duane Taylor, none of this would be coming to fruition without your support, love and mentorship. I thank you for all the advice, perspective, long conversations (thanks for always being willing to listen), and I appreciate your investment in my life and development. You are such an angel. Colleen, thank you for the long hours invested in editing this piece of work. Sir Doyle, Man, you've been there for me through the roughest times in my life and during the best! You are the epitome of a true friend/brother. Thank you for always being supportive, even when I felt I had no one else there.

I don't know how you deal with my craziness at times, but I thank you for it. Roger Stanley, my brother-you've always pushed me and kept. Me in a creative/productivemindset. I am thankful. Nijeul Porter, you really are the reason this project was completed. Thanks for your endless time, energy, expertise, the time lines you helped me create, thanks for being an accountability partner for me and always being honest and supportive of my ideas. You are a God-Send. Terrell Winder (thanks for always having my back and helping me make sense of my crazy mind and ideas). Darrell Mitchell (Big Brother), Thanks for always reading my work (way back in the days) and helping me bring it to life (now). I thank you for guiding me on this journey. Dr. David Malebranche, you've been a great inspiration and influence early on and I thank you for always being open and honest with me whenever I seek advice or perspective. Terrence Clemens, Man-we've jumped so many hurdles and conquered so much while supporting each other and I am blessed to have you in my corner. This is just the beginning. We have so much more to do-In Jesus name. Chris Cotton, Thank you for your insight, love and friendship. I look forward to seeing what you do next, it's very inspiring to watch you blossom my friend. Brennan Watson, thanks for all of the times you have talked sense into me when I was about to step outside of character and for always being consistent in your friendship. I got your back for life. Jamar Rogers, so many amazing moments, times of praise, dynamic conversations, and sharing our creativity. You are so inspiring and God truly does work through you. I love how close we have become and it feels good to know that we have each others friendship for a lifetime and more. People have no idea how brilliant you are, they've only been introduced to your gifts and talents, God has so much more for you. Tracy Kennedy, wow... Words cannot express how amazing our connection was. I am really sorry that you aren't here to really experience the release of a project you had been so supportive throughout. You and I had such a dope understanding, and you encouraged me to live my life and not stay so engulfed in work and everything else besides myself, because I would then live with regret. Reminding me that I am enough, and that I am amazing! (despite how others may have tried to make me feel). You helped me redefine what I wanted out of life, what makes me happy, and what it was that's stopped me. The times we would go eat and you would share your wisdom and perspective-#priceless. Always honest and transparent with me. Always loving and endearing. You will always be missed.RIP.Monica (@MonicaBrown), Everyone that knows me, knows how much I love me some Monica! What people may not know is that it surpasses your music, but it's your heart. The times when I felt no one seen me, understood me or could relate, I felt connected to you, and your music. I believe that God uses vessels/angels to connect and impact his children, and I feel that's what you were for me, an 'Angel of Mines'. I just thank you for your authenticity and each and every time we have met and spoken, you have been genuine, humble and sweet. All the more reason to love and support you even more. You have been a blessing in my life and I thank you! I will always support you and your music. God Bless you and your family.My Grandma (Janice Manley), Grandpa (Jesse Manley- RIP), Vergie, All of my Aunties, My Uncles, ALL of My Cousins, My Dads: Greg Cook and Joseph Hamilton, All of my brothers and sisters, nieces and nephews. Uncle Leroy Hamilton and fam. The entire Hamilton Family, The Duplechan Family, I love yaw so much! Jeffrey King, Phill Wilson, Terry Smith, Dr. Derek Greenfield, Michael Everett, Aunsha Hall, Gabe Maldonado, Donta Morrison, Darryl Lewis, Michelle Bennett, Peter Singleton, Sean Milan (Team-work always makes our dreams work), Jasmine McCloud-Thanks for doing an amazing job on my Book Cover design and art, Carla Gordon, Martha Chono-Helsley, Jeppe, Joe, Lawrence, Shannon Jones, Traci Bivens-Davis, Norma Barajas, Danielle Wondra, Tyreik Gaffney, Edward Smith, Allaire McDougall, Reneta McDougall, The McDougall family, Adriana Clark-Rambert, Devin McDaniel, Tori Towery, Kayla Hamilton, Donnie Frazier, Jerry Morris, Dr. Leo Moore, Malcolm Woods Jr., Brandon Fields, Amaya, Ronald Jackson, Tre' Jackson, William Johnson, Nicea Berry, Zella Gildon-Thank you for everything you have taught me...RIP, Charles Meats, ScottWimbley, Carolyn Martin, Amere Whitaker, Rodger Washington, Jamie (from LPCC), David Slack, Brandon Anthony, Chris Wilson, Gerald Garth, Robert Constantino, Norman Johnson, Jasmine McGruder, LaShawn Petus, Rosero McCoy, Chris Dunn, Arleta-(KT House), Barry Watson, Reggie Caldwell, Kellye McKenzie (NASTAD), Earl Wooten, DeJohn Chaffold, Nathan Eubanks, Demetrick Moore, Carl highshaw, Siri Sat Nam, Wayne Moody, Rev. Russell Thornhill, Eugene Smith, Tresvon Harville, Steve Hibbert, Ivanie Murphy-People still have no idea of how amazing your heartis. Yuriel Young, Joseph Wright, David McCoy, Charlie Parker, Richard Hamilton, Earl Wooten, Shane Jenkins, Quincey LaNear and Deondray Gossett. Ivan Daniel, Spencer Collins, Cynthia Brookins, Chris Blades, Stacy Alford, Devon Tomlin, Owen Sevier, Barrington Bell, Daunte Monroe, Kyle Gordon, Mervin Brandy, Slick!, Scott Hamilton, Mario Perez, Wayne Harris, Lance Blair, Junyur, Yiria, Danielle Rogers, Edward Carlington, Kieta, David D. Robertson, Jamaal Clue, Though there's a lot more people I would like to personally thank, I just wanted to list a few. If anyone's not mentioned that should be, charge my mind, not my heart. It was not intentional... Thanks for your support. I hope you enjoyed my 1st book!!!!! ☒ Get ready for the next ;)

Made in the USA
Las Vegas, NV
04 December 2020